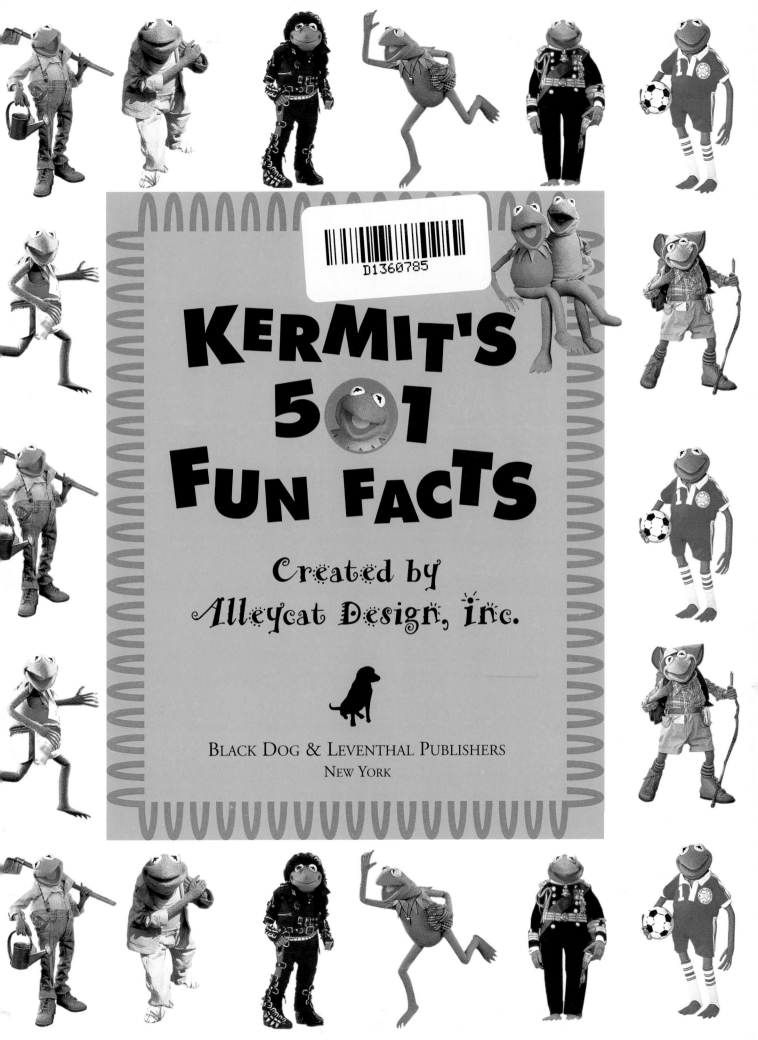

KERMIT'S 501 FUN FACTS

Created by
Alleycat Design, Inc.

BLACK DOG & LEVENTHAL PUBLISHERS
NEW YORK

ALL PHOTOGRAPHY BY JOHN E. BARRETT, EXCEPT:
David Dagley: Fact Nos. 27, 149, 404, 465, 487; Murray Close: Fact
Nos. 177, 362, 359, 414; Stephen F. Morley: Fact No. 112; Marcia Reed,
Sidney Baldwin, John Shannon: Fact No. 370.

Special thanks to Andrew Clements and Ellen Weiss
for their editorial contributions.

PUBLISHED BY
Black Dog & Leventhal Publishers, Inc.
151 West 19th Street
New York, NY 10011

DISTRIBUTED BY
Workman Publishing Company
708 Broadway
New York, NY 10003

TEXT BY DOUG CHILCOTT

ILLUSTRATIONS BY MYRON GROSSMAN AND STEVE TURK

Manufactured in the United States of America

ISBN: 1-884822-10-X

h g f e d c b a

LIBRARY OF CONGRESS CATALOGING-IN-PUBLICATION DATA
Chilcott, Doug.
Kermit's 501 fun facts/created by Alleycat Design; [text by Doug Chilcott].
p. cm.
Summary: Muppet photographs and color illustrations accompany facts about
mathematics, music, animals, vegetables, minerals, famous people, and more.
ISBN 1-884822-10-X
1. Curiosities and wonders—Juvenile literature. [1. Curiosities and wonders.]
I. Alleycat Design (Firm) II. Title.
AG243.C5447 1995
031.02—dc20   95-44275
CIP
AC

TABLE OF CONTENTS

RECORDS

1

Fast fly!
Ever try to outrun a dragonfly?

Good luck. They can fly as fast as 50 miles per hour!

biggest, smallest, longest, shortest, fastest, slowest

2

Blubberific . . .
The largest animal in the world is the blue whale. A blue whale can grow to be over 100 feet long and weigh more than 30 elephants!

But of course!

3

Vive la France . . . More people visit France each year than any other country in the world.

4

Favorite fizz . . .
The most popular soft drink in the world is Coca-Cola. Millions of people drink Coke every day. If you got to return all those cans and bottles, you'd be a millionaire!

5

Towering dino . . .
The tallest dinosaur we know of was the brachiosaurus branchi, or "lizard with arms." It stood over 39 feet tall, which means it could easily have peeked into a fourth-story window.

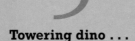

6

Golden oldie . . .
Your pet goldfish might live
as long as 30 or 40 years!

7

Big wheel . . .
The world's largest Ferris wheel is the Cosmolock 21 in
Yokohama City, Japan. It stands over 344 feet tall and is
328 feet wide.

8

Going, going, *gone*!
Hank Aaron is baseball's home
run king. He hit 755 home
runs — 41 more than Babe Ruth,
who is next in line
with 714.

9

"But I *am* hurrying . . . "
The slowest animal on earth is the
snail. At its fastest, the snail goes only
.03 miles an hour. That means it takes
almost a day-and-a half to go one mile.

12

Stink Blossom . . .
The world's largest flower is three
feet wide and weighs a whopping 15
pounds. It's called the rafflesia and grows
in the jungles of Southeast Asia. Its smell
is big, too—and awful. You would not
want to stick this flower in your
buttonhole!

10

Fasten your seat belts . . .
You are about to be lifted 207 feet—20 stories
—into the air and then hurled down a steep
hill. This is what awaits you if you ride the
world's tallest roller coaster, the Moonsault
Scramble, in Japan.

11

Wheee!
The first roller coasters were
built more than 300 years ago
in Russia. These coasters were
70–foot–high ice slides.

13

Walking into history . . .

He may not be the home run king anymore, but Babe Ruth still holds the record for walks. The Babe walked to first base 2,050 times in his 22-year career.

14 That's a lotta beef!

The McDonald's hamburger is the most popular sandwich in history. More than 8 billion of them have been sold so far. Side by side, these burgers would reach around the planet seven and a half times!

15

What's the largest city in the United States?

New York City? Los Angeles? No, it's Juneau, Alaska. Though Juneau doesn't have the most people, it has over six times more land than Los Angeles.

16

Super hooper . . .

Kareem Abdul-Jabbar has scored more points in basketball than any other player. He has scored 38,387 points in 1,560 games. That's an average of more than 24 points per game!

18

Long stretch . . . The Verrazano Narrows Bridge is one of the world's longest suspension bridges. It spreads more that two and a half miles over the entrance to New York Harbor.

17

Lots of Lego . . .

Can you imagine stacking Lego blocks twice as high as your house? Some people in Belgium did exactly that. They built the tallest Lego tower—70 feet high!

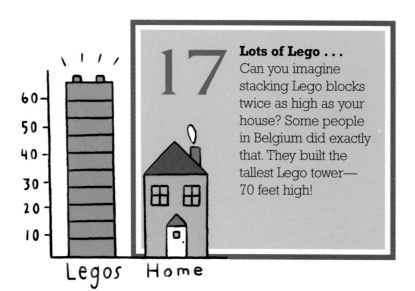

19

Big bird, indeed!
The albatross has the widest wingspan of any living bird. Even though its body is only nine inches wide, its wings stretch 11 feet from tip to tip.

21

Bats incredible . . .
The flying fox is the world's largest bat. Its wings spread over five feet.

20

Over the speed limit . . .
The fastest land animal would be pulled over for a speeding ticket if it were running on the highway. The quick-footed cheetah can run faster than 60 miles per hour.

23

Millions of bunnies . . .
The best–selling children's book of all time is *The Tale of Peter Rabbit* by Beatrix Potter. It has sold more than 9 million copies since it was first published in 1902.

22

Bigfoot is coming! The first of the *big* trucks was named Bigfoot, and it crushed its first car in 1981. Today, 14 different Bigfeet, along with lots of other big trucks, smash cars like bugs all over the country.

24

Like phoning 911 . . . The world's first telephone call was an emergency call. Alexander Graham Bell, the inventor of the telephone, spilled some battery acid on his pants as he was getting ready to test his invention. He called his assistant, saying, ''Watson, come here I want you!''

25

26

Roaches are forever . . .
Cockroaches are the oldest living species. They don't look much different now than they did 320 million years ago. They probably annoyed the dinosaurs, too!

But can he do the backstroke?
The fastest fish in the sea, the sailfish, can swim 65 miles per hour. A person at top speed swims five miles per hour.

As cold as a desert...
One of the world's largest deserts is also one of the coldest places on the planet. And the name of it is . . . Antarctica! Although it is covered with snow and ice, Antarctica gets only about four inches of new snow per year.

Oversized omelette . . .
If you'd like a hard-boiled ostrich egg for breakfast, you'd better set your alarm clock mighty early. It takes 40 minutes to boil a three-and-a-half-pound ostrich egg.

28

27

29

This tree's tops!
The world's tallest tree is so tall, you would almost expect to see a snowcap up there. At 368 feet, this giant redwood in California often has its top lost in the clouds.

Tongue–twister . . . If you'd like to send a postcard home from a certain lake in Massachusetts, you'd better buy a big one. It would have to say, "Greetings from Lake Chargoggagoggmanchauggagoggchaubunagungamaug." In Algonquin, the name means "You fish on your side, we fish on our side, nobody fishes in the middle." It's the longest place name in America.

Chargoggagoggmanchaugg

31

Feed me, Mom!

The biggest baby in the world eats so much that he gains 200 pounds a day! A baby blue whale is 23 feet long and weighs almost two tons shortly after birth.

32

It makes molasses look runny . . .
The slowest moving liquid in the world isn't ketchup. It's glass. Glass may look and feel like a solid, but it actually flows slowly over hundreds of years. If you visit an old house and look closely at the windows, you'll see that the glass at the bottom of each pane is thicker than the glass near the top.

33 Seen from above . . .
The longest wall in the world is the Great Wall of China. Built to keep out enemies, it is 1,500 miles long and stands 25 feet high. It is the only man-made structure that can be seen by astronauts orbiting the planet.

34 Speedy spider! The world's fastest spider doesn't come along. The sun spider of Africa chases down miles per hour. It's about three inches long and sit in a web and wait for lunch to lizards by running faster than 10 looks like a scorpion.

35

Zoom!
Our fastest creature might give Superman a good race. When an airborne peregrine falcon spots some food on the ground, it nose—dives at speeds of up to 200 miles per hour.

36 Tractor factor . . .
The wheels of the world's hugest tractors stand almost six feet high! They would make amazing tire swings if you could find a tree strong enough to hang them from.

goggchaubunagungamaug

What s

37

The CN Tower, Toronto, Ontario, Canada. World's tallest structure: 1,815 feet, 5 inches.

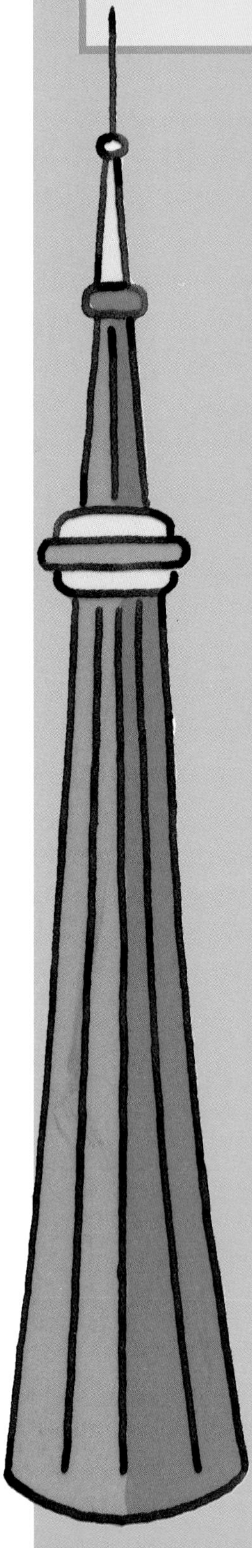

38

The Washington Monument, Washington, D.C.— 555 feet.

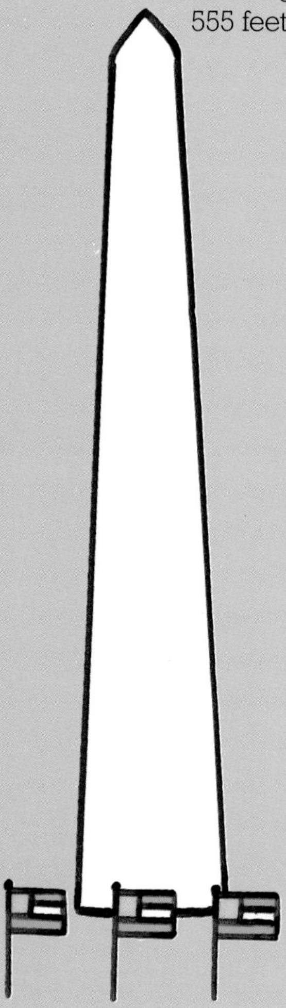

39

The Empire State Building, New York City. The tallest building in the world until 1973: 1,250 feet.

40

An average house 32 feet.

4

A tyrannosau rex: 20 feet.

taller?

43

A space shuttle on the launch pad: 184 feet.

The Sears Tower, Chicago, Illinois. World's tallest building: 1,454 feet.

42

The Eiffel Tower, Paris, France. The the tallest structure in the world until 1929: 984 feet.

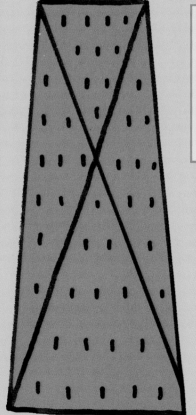

45

A giraffe: 18 feet.

46

A giraffe's neck: 7 feet.

47

The Great Pyramid of Cheops, Egypt: originally 481.4 feet. (The top 31 feet have been destroyed.)

48

False advertising . . .
There is nothing green about Greenland. The world's largest island is mostly covered with ice and snow. The Vikings called it Greenland to get people to move there.

49

The first computer filled a building the size of an average school. Today's smallest computer fits in your hand and is more powerful than even the first supercomputers.

50

Crowded place . . .
All of the people who live in Sweden, Finland, Norway, and Denmark could fit into the city of Tokyo, Japan.

Sweden
8,564,000

Norway
4,283,000

Finland
4,991,000

Denmark
5,134,000

52

Small room, big zoom...
It makes sense that the world's tallest building also has some of the speediest elevators. The elevators in Chicago's Sears Tower can whisk you from the lobby to the 103rd floor in just 45 seconds.

53

Power towers . . .
Every person in Erie, Pennsylvania, could fit into the World Trade Center. Some 50,000 people work in its five buildings, and another 70,000 visit every day.

51

Umbrellas wouldn't help . . .
The rainiest day ever was on the island of Reunion, off the Indian Ocean. It rained more than 73 inches in 24 hours. Even on a very wet day, it's unusual to get more than two inches of rain anywhere in the world.

54

Better bring a bike . . .
The worlds largest office building is only five stories high. It is the Pentagon, in Washingtn, D.C. If you walked down every hallway of this five–sided building, you would walk 17 and a half miles.

55

A long way down . . .
Angel Falls in Venezuela is the tallest waterfall in the world. At its highest point, it is 3,212 feet high—or more than 20 times taller than Niagara Falls.

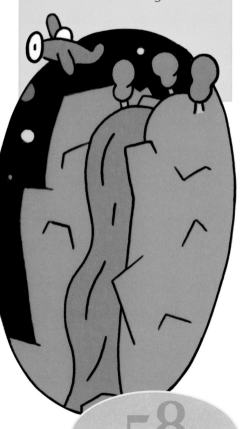

57

Quit shoving!
Tokyo has the world's most crowded trains. At rush hour, the subways are so jammed that there are people whose job it is to shove everyone into the cars so the doors can close.

56

One-man team?
Wilt Chamberlain scored 100 points in a basketball game on March 2, 1962, playing for the Philadelphia Warriors. It is the most points ever scored by a single player in an NBA game.

58

Shell shock . . .
How big can the world's biggest turtle get? Pretty big: The shell of a leatherback turtle can be as large as a king-size bed.

AMAZING ANIMALS

60 Beeware . . .

The next time a bee buzzes by, take a good look. It may be a fly. The drone fly looks and sounds like a bee, but it doesn't have a stinger. It just wants you to think it's a bee so you'll leave it alone.

59 Coat trick . . .

The snowshoe hare has a special coat. In the winter, its fur changes from brown to white to blend in with the snow. In the spring and summer, its fur becomes brown again, so it can blend in with the colors of the forest.

61 Large litter . . .

People think that having one baby is a big job, but . . . a mother pig can have as many as 27 babies at one time!

63 Useful tooth . . .

Reptiles and birds have an "egg tooth" to help them break open their shells. The egg tooth falls off soon after the animal hatches.

62 Sneak attack . . .

A crocodile sneaks up on its prey like a submarine. Its eyes are on top of its head so it can see as it glides silently toward its next meal.

64 Yahoo, spideroo!

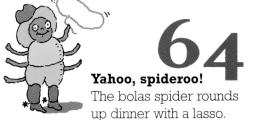

The bolas spider rounds up dinner with a lasso. First it spins a silky, sticky rope. When it sees a moth, it uses its front legs to swing the rope around and rein in the moth. *Bolas* is the Spanish word for a lasso.

65

Shoveler . . .
The word *caribou*
means "shoveler." This kind
of reindeer got its name
because it finds its
winter food by
shoveling away the
snow with its hooves.

66

Show time!
The male
bowerbird of Australia arranges a
collection of silvery twigs into something
that looks like a piece of artwork. He
tries to attract a female bowerbird to his
creation, hoping she'll build her nest
nearby.

67

Godzilla? The komodo dragon is the largest and most
ferocious lizard in the world. It can grow to be 10 feet long,
and attacks deer and wild boar. It has
been known to attack and kill
people, too. Today the komodo
dragon is an endangered species and
can be found only on four small islands in
Southeast Asia.

68

Equal partners . . . Mother
and father chinstrap penguins
take turns sitting on their eggs.
When the babies hatch, the one
that was siting on them at the
time waddles down to the water to fill up on
the small shrimp called krill and brings a nice
batch back   for the babies.

Below-zero hero . . .
A dog once saved an entire city. In the
winter of 1925, many people in Nome,
Alaska, got sick and needed medicine
from another town. It was snowing so
hard that the only way to get help was
by dogsled. The sled driver got lost in
the blowing snow, but a dog named
Balto led the way and got the medicine back to Nome in time to save the
village. A statue of Balto stands in
Central Park in New York City.

69

70

Ready, aim, phew!
A skunk can aim its stinky smell
at something 12 feet away!

Amazing Animals

Looks like big trouble! When a puffer fish gets scared, it doesn't swim away–it has a drink! It quickly swallows lots of water, puffing itself up into a huge ball to scare away fish twice its size.

71

Fishin' fishies . . .

Who ever heard of a fish going fishing? That's what the anglerfish does every day. It dangles a bit of bait from a natural fishing line that grows out of its head. Smaller fish go for the bait, and then the angler-fish reels them in.

Ocean treasure . . .

A pearl is formed when a scratchy piece of sand or grit gets caught inside the shell of an oyster or mussel. To protect itself from this bothersome sand, the mollusk covers the tiny object with layer after layer of a substance called nacre. After enough layers are built up, the pearl is complete.

Underwater Einstein . . .

The octopus is one of the smartest creatures in the sea. It can even learn how to unscrew the lid on a glass jar to get at the tasty crab inside.

74

Let me out!

75

Strolling . . .

A fish out of water isn't always uncomfortable. The walking catfish can live out of the water for a few days. It walks by using its side fins.

76

Shark radar . . . A shark can "hear" your heartbeat a mile away. A special sixth sense enables the shark to pick up electrical pulses. Your heart gives off this kind of energy with every beat.

77 **Toothy grin . . .**
Do you know how a shark's teeth stay so sharp? The teeth are constantly falling out as sharper new ones grow in. A shark can have up to 30,000 teeth in its lifetime.

78

Ptoooey! Sharks don't like the way we taste. When a shark attacks a person, it takes one bite and spits it out. It would rather eat a fish or a seal.

79

Gentler sharks . . .
Not all sharks are scary. Some kinds have small teeth, and they eat only tiny fish and plankton, which are the nearly invisible plants and animals that float in ocean water.

Today's MENU
✓ Sealion
✓ Octopus
✓ Barracuda
✓ Devilfish
✓ Tigerfish

No one here but us sponges . . . Some animals put on disguises to hide. The sponge crab uses its claw to cut a little jacket out of a sponge. It slips on the sponge jacket and holds it in place with a special set of legs. A predator looking for a crab will swim past this one because it looks like a sponge.

Amazing Animals

81 Super sucker . . .
An octopus has 240 powerful suction cups on each one of its eight arms. If they grab hold, good luck getting loose.

82 No rain? No problem!
The gerbil is also known as the sand rat, and it's the camel of the rodent family. Some varieties can survive in the desert for nearly a year without water.

83 Safely hidden . . .
The xenophora is a shellfish that dresses up as a pile of underwater junk. It makes a special kind of goo to glue bits and pieces of shells, rocks, and other things to its shell.

84 Music to her ears . . .
Only male frogs make the famous "ribbet" sound. They croak to attract female frogs.

86 Sneaky, Snaky tongue . . .
An anteater's tongue can be over two feet long! It uses it to reach into an ant's nest and eat dinner.

85 Frightful frog . . .
The giant, or Goliath, frog is the world's largest frog. The over-sized tadpoles grow up into frogs that can stretch one whole foot from head to tail. When someone tried to enter one in the world frog-jumping championships, it was too big to fit on the starting pad.

87

Dancing for food . . .
When a bee finds food, it returns to the beehive and dances, to tell the others how to get to the food. The faster the bee dances, the further away the food is.

89

Bee cool . . . To cool down in the hive on hot days, bees turn on the air-conditioning—their own kind, of course. Workers line up near the entrance to the hive and fan the air with their wings.

88

Chubby cheeks . . .
Hamsters got their name from the German word *hamstern,* which means "to hoard." The hamster packs extra food into its bulging cheeks and carefully hides extra food all over its cage.

90

Huge hunger . . .
A blue whale eats 550 pounds of food every day. As you might guess, it spends lots of time looking for breakfast, lunch, dinner, and snacks.

91

Spider serenade . . .
Some male spiders pluck the strands of their webs like guitar strings to get the attention of female spiders.

93

Peepers . . .
A giant squid has the largest eyes of any animal yet discovered. Its eyes are bigger than dinner plates.

92

Birth announcement . . . When a porpoise is born, other female porpoises hear the mother's whistle and come to snuggle with the new baby.

Amazing Animals

95
Stand and snooze . . .
Horses and cows have a special kind of knee joint. When they stand still on all four legs, their legs stay straight and stiff. Beds with four stiff legs don't fall over, and neither do cows and horses. So these large animals don't have to lie down to rest. They can just stand still and fall fast asleep.

94
No batteries required . . .
The rooster likes to begin his day by telling the world that he is the boss of his barnyard. His piercing wake-up call comes with the first faint beam of sunlight—or even earlier!

96

Shear warmth . . .
Every spring, sheep get haircuts—and not just a trim, either. It's an all over haircut called shearing. A sheep's soft wool is used to make yarn that gets turned into sweaters and mittens and hats.

97
No kidding . . .
Baby goats are called kids. Sound familiar? Mother goats produce milk that's good for their kids, just as mother humans produce milk that's good for *their* kids.

98
Old MacDonald had a . . . trout?

Don't laugh. Salmon, trout, and some kinds of shellfish are grown on watery, man-made farms in a process called aquaculture.

Two-course meal . . .
A cow likes its dinner so much that it eats it twice. That's because it has two stomachs. First, the cow munches on tough grass and hay, and swallows it into stomach number one. After the stomach has softened the lump of food awhile, it comes back up into the cow's mouth to be chewed again. That lump of food is called cud, and the second time it is swallowed, it goes to the second stomach to be fully digested.

99

101

Milk marvel . . .
An average American cow produces 1,780 gallons of milk each year.

100

MILK

We'd rather be swimming . . .
Pigs don't love dirt. They wallow in mud to cool off when it gets too hot. If a clean pool of water is available, pigs prefer that over mud any day.

102

Super chickens?
Some modern farms are run like factories. Hens kept in cages in laying houses can produce eggs quickly and cheaply because all the conditions—light and heat and food—can be controlled. The eggs are even collected automatically! But recently, people have started to ask if this kind of farming is fair to the animals.

Amazing Animals

103

Pant, pant . . .
A dog pants to cool itself down. It exhales hot, moist air and breathes in cool air. Dogs sweat only through their tongues!

105

No need for wigs!
Bald eagles aren't bald. Their head of white feathers just makes them look that way.

104 **Don't yawn, Dad!**

After a female Darwin frog lays her eggs, the male stores them in a pouch in his mouth. They don't get in the way of his eating, and soon they hatch into tadpoles. They hang around in their dad's mouth until they shed their tails and jump out as young hoppers.

106

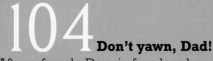

Tooth trouble . . .
Rabbits and guinea pigs have teeth that never stop growing. In the wild, they chew on wood constantly, and this keeps their teeth worn down to a useful size. If they eat only soft foods, their teeth grow longer and longer until they can't close their mouths.

107

Blink, Blink—Hi!
Since they can't speak, fireflies meet and talk to each other by flicking their lights on and off.

108

Spider sailor . . .
The raft spider of Great Britain sets sail for dinner every night. It builds a boat out of dead leaves and then cruises around looking for insects.

109

Escape artist . . . When it is scared, an octopus squirts out a cloud of dark, inky fluid that clouds the water and sometimes even paralyzes its attacker. And where is the octopus when the water clears? Long gone.

110

It's a wing thing . . . The buzzing sound of bees, flies, and flying beetles is made by the rapid beating of their wings. And that high-pitched whine that a mosquito makes? Its wings can beat up to 500 times in a second.

111

Born to jump . . . With a running start, a mature kangaroo can jump the full length of a school bus—over 45 feet!

112

No cola for a koala . . . Koala bears are probably the fussiest eaters in the world. They eat only the leaves from eucalyptus trees. They don't even drink water. In fact, the word *koala* means "no water."

113

Crabby clockwork . . . The fiddler crab lives on the beach. When the tide comes in, it burrows under the sand. It has a built-in timer that tells it when the tide is coming. Even if the fiddler crab is taken away from the beach and lives in a tank, its timer keeps working, and it hides during what would be high tide.

HOW THINGS WORK

115

Join me! When a bone breaks, it needs time to "glue" itself back together. A doctor puts a plaster cast around the place where the break happened to hold the bone ends in place while they heal.

114 The one and only you . . .
There are at least two ways that you are different from every other person on earth. Your fingerprints and your voice are unique, and can be used to identify you. That's why detectives are always looking for fingerprints at the scenes of crimes. Scientists are also able to identify a person's "voiceprint"—the particular shape of the soundwaves that your voice makes.

116

Sweat slurper . . .
If you sweat in space, you need a vacuum cleaner to remove the sweat from your skin. In zero gravity, it sticks.

Bone shadows . . . An X ray isn't a picture of your bones. It is your skeleton's shadow. The part of your body that the doctor wants to look at is put in front of a piece of film that is sensitive to X-ray radiation. This radiation is like a light that can shine through skin and soft tissue, but it can't shine through bones.

118

A peek at a peak . . .
If you've ever visited an island in the ocean, then you've been to the top of a mountain. An island is actually the top of a mountain sticking up from the ocean floor.

117

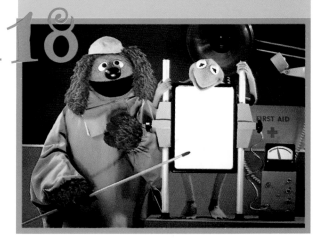

119 Prehistoric clues . . .

Fossils are imprints of the bodies of prehistoric plants and animals that were somehow covered with soil or mud or ash before they decomposed. Fossils are some of the best clues we have about what life was like on earth millions of years ago.

120

What goes up . . .

Helium balloons float into the air simply because helium gas weighs less than the air outside the balloon.

121

Air cushion . . .

A hovercraft doesn't ride on tires, it blows air down toward the ground and actually lifts itself a few feet into the air. Sitting atop this cushion of air, the hovercraft can glide quickly over water or land.

122

Summer cover-up . . .

The red and orange colors you see in autumn leaves have always been there. During the spring and summer, the green color is so strong that it covers up the other colors. When the trees get ready for winter, green liquid called chlorophyl stops flowing into the leaves. When it is gone, you can see the other colors.

123

Nothing to digest . . .

Your body gets used to eating meals at certain times of the day. Even if you don't eat, your stomach acts as though you have. It grumbles and gurgles because it has started to do its normal work on a meal, but the meal isn't there to work on!

124 Compass pointers . . .

A compass needle always points north because it's really a little magnet that can swing freely. The "north" pole of the needle, marked with an *N*, is attracted to a huge magnetic force at the earth's North Pole.

125

Plant plumbing. . .

In most plants, the roots do the drinking for the whole plant. Then they pump water up through tiny plant pipes, or veins, to keep the stem, leaves, and flowers supplied. If you hold a leaf up to the light, you can see its veins.

126

Nice paint job . . . Through most of your life, your body sends a kind of "paint" called pigment to your hair. When the paint runs out, your hair stops looking black, brown, red, or blond, and grows gray or white.

127

Onion alert! An onion makes you cry because when you cut into it, you release a gas that irritates your eyes. To wash this gas away, your eyes fill with tears. It's kind of like washing your car windshield.

128

Red as a lobster . . . A sunburn is an injury to your skin. The sun's rays make the blood vessels in your skin open wider so you have more blood in your skin. That's what makes it turn red. These harmful rays may also make your skin swell and blister. Always remember to wear sun block!

130

Longer and lower . . . Your voice is created by the vibration of chords at the back of your throat. These vocal chords grow along with the rest of your body. Your voice changes because the length of the vocal chords changes. The longer they grow, the lower and deeper your voice becomes.

129

Sneeze warning . . . A sneeze is your body's way of getting rid of something it doesn't want . . . fast! Your nose tells your brain that something is bothering it. The brain's response is that ticklish feeling in your nose that quickly turns into a sneeze.

131

Nose power . . . A good sneeze can be powerful. Particles from a sneeze have been clocked at speeds over 100 miles per hour!

132 ZZZZZZZZZ . . .

A sleeping person snores when he breathes through the mouth instead of the nose. A flap of skin at the back and top of the mouth vibrates and makes the sound we call snoring. Adult men are much more likely to snore than women or children are.

133

Sharper image . . . Your eyes work like a camera. A lens focuses on an object and projects an image onto a small "screen" inside the eye. The brain gets the signal and "develops" the picture you see. When what you see is fuzzy, a pair of glasses can refocus the blurry image so that the brain gets a sharp, clear picture again.

134

Face facts . . .
It takes 14 different muscles to smile and
20 different muscles to frown. So if you're
feeling tired, you should smile—
it's easier!

136

Eyewashers . . . You are always crying,
even when you aren't sad. Your eyes are
constantly being washed with fresh tears.
Sadness or other strong emotions can
send a rush of tears into your eyes so that
they overflow and run down your face.

135

Help from the skin . . .
Your body's largest organ is clearly
visible without an X ray—your skin!
One of the skin's most important jobs
is helping regulate your temperature.
If you start to get cold, reactions from
the skin will make you shiver, and the
muscle activity from shivering can
help warm you up. And if you get too
warm, the skin sweats. As the sweat
evaporates, you cool down.

137

Taste test . . .
The front of your tongue loves sugar. The back just can't get enough of salty popcorn. Each of the 3,000 taste
buds on your tongue is sensitive to a special taste—bitter, salt, sweet, or sour. When you eat something,
the different flavors "wake up" the taste buds that like them.

138 Lazy winter . . .

Fish can't travel to warmer places for the winter the way many birds do. But don't worry, they don't freeze. Most ponds and lakes are only frozen on top. To get through the winter, the fish relax, swim more slowly, and hardly eat at all.

Do, re, mi . . .

The longer a musical instrument, the lower the sound that comes out of it. When you cover the holes on a flute, the air has to travel farther before it comes out, so the sound gets lower.

139 Hidden code . . .

That little computer "bar code" that you see on everything from candy wrappers to cereal boxes has a story to tell. If you were a laser computer scanner, it might tell you the name of the item it appears on, how much the item costs, what color it is, or what company made it—or all of those things.

7210326

140

141 Breathing bread . . .

When you make bread dough, the yeast reacts with the starch and sugar to produce a gas called carbon dioxide. As the gas "breathes" thousands of tiny bubbles into the mass, the dough rises. Look carefully at a slice of bread, and you'll see hundreds of tiny bubbles.

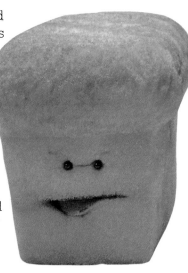

142 Water scooting . . .

When you go ice-skating, you are really skating on water. The blade of your skate applies the pressure of your body weight to the ice. This creates friction and heat, which together melt a thin layer of ice. This water on top of the ice is what makes you glide so easily.

144

Sun source . . . The fuel that runs the sun is hydrogen. The sun uses 4 million tons of hydrogen every second. But don't worry about it running out of gas. It has enough in the tank to run for at least 5 billion more years.

143

Sun sensitive . . .

No matter where in a room you put a plant, its leaves always turn toward the sun. Leaves need light to make their own food as they grow. They can sense where the most light comes from, and slowly, their leaves turn in that direction.

Monster magnet . . .
Even a tiny magnet can be a monster to a computer disk. The information stored on a disk is like millions of tiny magnetic "on and off switches" set in a precise pattern. Moving a magnet near the disk is like flipping all the buttons every which way. The pattern is ruined and the damage is done.

145

146 Sticky business . . .
A spiderweb has sticky threads that trap flies and bugs, but the spider itself never gets stuck. How come? Because the spider also weaves in a network of *nonsticky* threads. It walks on these. And even if it slips off, a spider's legs are covered with an oil that won't stick to even the sticky parts.

147

Dirt magnet . . .

Soap acts like a magnet that attracts opposites. When soap combines with water, it attracts dirt. When you rinse off the soap, it carries the dirt away with the rinse water, and all that's left behind are your clean hands.

148

What's up, what's down . . . Thanks to gravity, a tiny seed buried deep in the ground always knows where to reach for the sunshine. The plant's roots are the first things to grow, and gravity pulls them down toward the center of the earth. The rest of the plant always grows in the opposite direction— up to the sunlight.

A lesson from a log . . . Nature is good at using things over again. When a tree dies, it falls to the ground and rots, becoming food for insects, which become food for birds, which become food for bigger birds and foxes, which can build their dens inside the rotten log. But many of the things people make only get used once, and then they sit in a landfill for hundreds of years. Recycling is a way for us to reuse things we've made so we don't waste energy or fill up the planet with trash.

Recycled water . . . The water you brushed your teeth with this morning could have been the same water that a dinosaur sipped with dinner more than 150 million years ago. The earth uses the same water over and over again. It evaporates into the atmosphere, condenses into clouds, and comes down as rain, sleet, hail, or snow. It then runs into rivers, lakes, and oceans. After that, it starts its journey all over again. And it's still the very same water!

151

150

Letting off steam . . . Far below the surface of the earth, it is so hot that rocks melt. When parts of the earth's crust move during an earthquake, sometimes steam and gasses and ashes and hot lava burst from the opening and form a volcano. There are more than 850 active volcanoes around the world today.

152 **Shaky ground . . .** Earthquakes happen every day. That's because the surface of the earth, even the part that's underwater, is like a big eggshell with lots of cracks. The different pieces of the shell, or crust, are constantly shifting. When they make a large or sudden shift, everything near that spot shakes and rumbles. Fortunately, most earthquakes are small and happen deep down on the ocean floor.

153

Platelets to the rescue . . .
When you get a cut, your body sets up its own roadblock to stop the bleeding. Tiny agents in your blood, called platelets, quickly build a dam to block the blood. When you see a scab on a cut, that's dried-up platelets.

Huff and puff that oxy stuff . . . When you

154

run around the block, you breathe faster and faster. Your body needs air just as a car needs gas. When you exercise, your muscles call for more of the energy stored in your body, and that energy-using process needs oxygen. When you stop using so much energy, your breathing returns to normal.

155

That's how we shed, Fred . . .
You may change your clothes every day, but did you know that your whole body changes its outfit? We shed little particles of skin all the time. About every four weeks, an entirely new layer of skin has replaced the old one!

156

Pins and needles . . .
Your hand or foot "falls asleep" because it isn't getting the blood it needs. If you sit on your foot for a long time, your body can't pump enough blood to keep it working properly, and your foot begins to tingle. When you move and let the blood flow, that "pins and needles" feeling gets stronger as the blood rushes back, and then the feeling slowly goes away as your foot "wakes up."

157

Bumps for warmth . . . Did you ever wonder why you get goose bumps? Here's what happens. The hairs on your skin are connected to tiny muscles, called arrector muscles. These muscles tighten up when you get cold or scared. That's what makes the hair stand up, forming goose bumps.

158

Fast food? Not on the inside . . . It takes your body almost two days to digest one meal!

159
Moving pictures . . .
A movie is actually thousands and thousands of still photos flashed quickly onto the screen, one after another. They go by so fast that your eyes cannot keep up with them. Since each picture is slightly different from the one just before it, it looks like the people and things are moving—which is why films are called movies.

160
Hot stuff . . . When something gets warmer, it expands. The liquid inside a thermometer spreads out as it gets warmer, moves up the tube, and reaches the higher numbers.

161
A new wrinkle . . . Did you ever wonder why older people have wrinkles in their skin? Skin is a lot like a rubber band. It is always being stretched back and forth. And like a rubber band, the skin gets tired of stretching and stops snapping back the way it used to. When the skin loses elasticity, wrinkles appear.

I 62
From friction into flame . . .
When you rub your hands together, the heat that you feel comes from friction. Matches use friction, too. When a kitchen match is rubbed on a rough surface, this produces heat from friction. A chemical, called sulphur, at the tip of the match catches fire easily, and the match is lit.

163
Muscle power . . . Your muscles are a lot like the strings on a puppet. They lift and move your bones so you can walk or stretch or scratch your nose.

164

Weigh less fast!
Astronauts weigh less on the Moon because the Moon is smaller than the earth. Your weight is based on the pull of gravity, and a planet's gravity is based on its size and mass. The Moon has one-sixth the gravitational pull of the earth, because it has one-sixth the mass of the Earth. That means that if an astronaut weighs 180 pounds on Earth, he will weigh only one-sixth of that—30 pounds—on the Moon. How much would *you* weigh on the Moon?

165

Sea sounds . . .
When you put your ear up to a sea shell, it sounds like the ocean. But what you are really hearing is air blowing through the shell. You may also be hearing the sound of blood being pumped through your ear, because the shell is trapping the sound and reflecting it back to you.

166 Burnout . . .
The clink you hear when you shake a burned-out lightbulb is a broken piece of wire—the filament. In a lightbulb, electricity going through a filament gets it so hot that it lights up. After a while, the wire weakens, and when it breaks, the bulb burns out.

168

Eavesdropping . . .
If you put the bottom of a drinking glass against a wall and then put your ear inside the open end, you can hear what's happening in the next room. A stethoscope works the same way, only the next room is inside your heart!

167

Blow out, suck in . . .
A vacuum cleaner is just a powerful blower between two openings. It blows air out the back opening, and that creates a vacuum, which makes air rush into the front opening where the hose is hooked on. And along with all the air comes the dust and dirt. The dirty stuff gets trapped in a bag and your carpet gets clean.

169

Popcorn! Corn kernels have a clear, hard covering around them. When a kernel is heated, the moisture inside starts turning to steam. The pressure builds up and up and up until—*pop!* It breaks open. When that happens, the starchy inside of the kernel bursts out, all white and fluffy.

SPORTS

Games & Fun

171

Do Dodgers dodge?
Ever wonder what the Los Angeles Dodgers are supposed to dodge? Years ago, when the team was started in Brooklyn, New York streetcars raced up and down the crowded streets. People from Brooklyn were nicknamed trolley dodgers, and that's where the team got its name.

170

But don't try this at home! A ski jumper looks as if he is soaring hundreds of feet up in the air. Actually, the jumper is rarely more than 10 feet off the ground—which is the height of the jump ramp. He may descend several hundred feet, but he's just following the downward slope of the mountain.

172

Baseball's sign language . . .
The first umpires only yelled their calls: "Strike!" "Safe!" "You're Out!" Hand signals were added in 1890, so that a deaf outfielder named William Hoy could follow the game better.

173

Quite a spectacle . . .
Henry Pullman of Holland ran the 1987 New York City Marathon wearing wooden shoes, a wheel of cheese on his head, and toy windmills on his shoulders.

Elephant game . . .
In 1976, in Jaipur, India, elephant polo was born. It's a much slower game than the one played with quick-footed polo ponies, and the mallets are almost twice as long. Grabbing the ball with a trunk is strictly forbidden!

175

Which twin will win?
One of the closest ski races in Olympic history was between twin brothers. Phil Mahre of the United States beat his brother, Steve, by fractions of a second and won the gold medal in the 1984 Winter Olympics men's slalom.

Jumpy judges . . . In the 1920 Olympics, Theresa Weld of the United States was the first woman figure skater to attempt a jump in competition. The judges reduced her scores because jumping was considered unladylike, but she still won a gold medal.

176

Pedal to the medal . . .
The world's longest bicycle race is the Race Across America. The course stretches from Irvine, California, to Savannah, Georgia—2,910 miles.

177

178

Soggy hockey . . .
In South Africa, a hockey face-off can happen at the bottom of a swimming pool. In a game called octopush, players wearing scuba gear and flippers play hockey on the floor of a pool.

179

Birth of the belly flop . . .
The first divers were gymnasts looking for softer landings. In Germany and Sweden during the 1600s, gymnasts began practicing at the beach. A goof-up over the water didn't hurt as much as a flub over the ground.

180

Sky pies . . .
The first Frisbees came with pies inside them. Students at Yale University invented the flying disk after throwing around empty pie pans from the Frisbie Pie Company of New Haven, Connecticut. The design changed, the name changed a little . . . and bingo!

181
Girls want to have fun, too!
The first women's World Cup soccer tournament took place in China in November 1991—61 years after the men's World Cup began. The United States beat Norway, 2 to 1.

182
Guilty!
Soccer was so popular in England that in the 12th century, King Henry II outlawed it. He was afraid that his army was playing too much, and hoped they'd practice shooting arrows instead of goals. Soccer remained illegal in England for the next 400 years.

183
The pen is mightier than the sword—unless the sword *is* a pen . . .
Fencers always wear white uniforms. In the old days, each sword was dipped in ink. Any touches of the opponent's sword left inky marks that made scorekeeping easy. Today, sensors built into each player's uniform pick up any touches electronically. En garde!

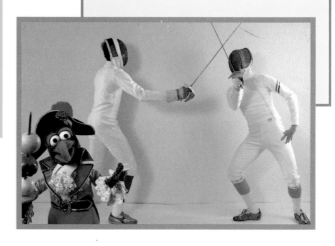

184
No need for lockers . . .
In Greek, the word *gymnasium* means "to exercise naked." Care to guess what the ancient Greeks wore when they played their sports?

185
Better than windshield wipers . . .
Before a horse race, the jockey puts on several pairs of goggles. During the race, the horses kick up so much dirt and mud that the goggles are soon covered. So the jockey just rips off the dirty goggles, and he or she can see again—until *that* pair gets dirty.

186
A king in trouble . . .
Chess was invented in ancient Asia, and the term *checkmate* can be traced back to those times. In Persia, the king was called the shah. *Shah-mat* meant "the shah is helpless." *Checkmate* still means that the king cannot move except into more danger.

Hey, this thing *bounces!*
Under the original 1892 rules, no player could "carry the ball." The basketball was passed or handed from player to player to get it to the basket. In 1896, it was decided that a player could move the ball forward as long as he was bouncing it, and dribbling was born.

188

187 **War game . . .** Carousels began as part of a game called "little war," played in Arabia 900 years ago. Soldiers rode their horses around in a circle and passed a ball. Soon the game was played in Europe. To practice, players mounted wooden horses on a rack that revolved, and the merry-go-round was born.

The wrestling presidents . . .
When he wasn't busy chopping down cherry trees, George Washington liked to wrestle. He is one of seven wrestling presidents, including Abraham Lincoln and Teddy Roosevelt.

189

Barbecue ball . . . A football field is known as "the gridiron" because all those yardlines and sidelines make it look like a huge barbecue grill. Did some hungry fans come up with that idea?

191

190

Little no more . . . Little League baseball was founded in 1939, with just a handful of kids. It is now played in 33 countries by more than 2 million boys and girls. The Little League World Series is held each fall in Williamsport, Pennsylvania—the town where it all began.

Sports, Games & Fun

185 miles per hour

A sky diver falling to earth.

170 miles per hour

A golf ball off the tee.

192

193

25 miles per hour

Fastest running speed, Carl Lewis, 1984 Olympic sprint relays

194

195 138 miles per hour

Fastest serve in tennis, by Steve Denton of Australia on July 29, 1984.

196 **188 miles per hour**

A ball in jai alai — the fastest ball in sports.

197

50.84 miles per hour

Fastest cyclist, Fred Markham, in Ontario, California, on May 6, 1979.

198

186 miles per hour

Fastest average speed record in the Indianapo[...]
set by Arie Luyendyk in 1990.

199

80 miles per hour

Fastest luge run,
by Asle Strand of Norway
on May 1, 1982.

200

Slow going . . . A badminton shuttlecock, or "birdie," can go this fast– *200 miles per hour*– but only for a fraction of a second. No matter how hard you whack it, the little feathers act like a mini-parachute and slow it down almost instantly.

How Fast — Does It Go?

201

Fastest speed on skis: 129 miles an hour, in April 1994.

319 miles per hour

202

Fastest speedboat, the *Spirit of Australia*, piloted by Ken Warby in October 1978.

203

Speed of a surfer racing down a huge
wave, 35 miles and hour.

THE ORIGIN

204
Badminton

My house, my game . . .
Badminton is based on a game brought to England from India during the 1800s. Originally called poona, it was popular at the home of the duke of Beaufort. And the name of his grand manor house? Badminton.

205
Lacrosse

Lacrossing the country . . . Lacrosse is the oldest team sport in North America, dating back to the time before Columbus came to the New World. The Native Americans called it baggataway, which means "little brother of war," and they played the game to settle their differences. These early games had as many as 1,000 men on each side, could last for up to three days, and the goals would sometimes be miles apart.

206
Table Tennis

Corking good time . . .
The first game of table tennis took place in 1879, when two students at England's Cambridge University began hitting a champagne cork back and forth over a pile of books on a table. For paddles they used empty cigar boxes.

207
They could've called it boink-boink . . .
Table tennis has become known as ping-pong because *ping* is the sound of the paddle hitting the ball, and *pong* is the sound of the ball hitting the table.

208
Hockey

Duck—a puck!
The best guess is that hockey—like lacrosse—originated with the Iroquois. They played a similar game in the 1700s, hitting a hard ball across a field with sticks. When someone was hit by the ball, he shouted "Ho-gee!" which means "It hurts!"   Sounds like hockey, don't you think?

HO-GEE!

209
Soccer

Head games . . . An old story about the origin of the game of soccer has a gruesome twist. It seems that England was at war with Denmark, and a British soldier took the skull of a Danish soldier and began kicking it around a level field. Years later, when the skull had been replaced by a soccer ball, many folks still called the game "kick the Dane's head."

210
Golf

Herding and hitting . . .
Golf was invented by shepherds in Scotland. They used their crooked wooden staffs to hit roc[k] and pebbles into rabbit holes.

211

OF SPORTS

Baseball

British beanball . . . One of the games that led to baseball is the English game called rounders. As in baseball, a batter hits the ball and runs "round" a set of bases—but clockwise, the opposite direction of a baseball runner. And the way to put the runner out in rounders? Just throw the ball right at him! Baseball added the less painful method of tagging runners at the bases.

212

The Marathon

Good news travels fast . . . The modern marathon celebrates the legendary run of a Greek soldier in the year 490 B.C. He ran more than 24 miles, from the battlefield at Marathon to Athens, to bring the good news of victory. It wasn't until the 1926 Olympics that the official marathon distance became 26 miles, 385 yards.

214

Basketball

Name that game . . . Basketball might have been boxball. In 1891, James Naismith was looking for a game to play indoors and thought it might be fun to throw balls into boxes. But he could only find peach baskets. He nailed the baskets to the walls 10 feet above the floor of a gymnasium in Springfield, Massachusetts, and tossed in a soccer ball. Today's rims still hang at the same height as those first peach baskets.

213 Tennis

Check out my backhand . . . Tennis is based on a French game called *jeu de paume*, "game of the palm." Instead of rackets, players used their hands to hit the ball over the net.

216

A league of their own . . .

Women were not allowed to compete in the original Olympic Games in ancient Greece. So they formed their own sporting games and called them Heraea, after the Greek goddess Hera. These games had only one event, a running race.

215

Hopping through history . . .

The oldest hopscotch board in the world is carved into the stone floor of the Forum in Rome.

217

Crash!

In 1760, a Belgian inventor named Joseph Merlin demonstrated his newest brainchild: roller skates. Unfortunately, he lost control and crashed through a huge plate-glass window. It wasn't a very good beginning and roller skates were not introduced to the public again until many years later.

218

King Pong . . .

A robot is helping train the U.S. table tennis team. It can shoot a ping-pong ball as fast as 60 miles per hour. The robot has a wicked spin, and it can hit any spot on the table. And it never hits the net!

219

Fast female . . .

In 1977, Janet Guthrie became the first woman to race in the Indianapolis 500.

Fourscore and seven *aggies* ago?

Young Abe Lincoln was good at a lot of things— he liked chopping contests, foot races, and wrestling matches. But one of his very favorite games was marbles.

220

221

Funny money . . .

More than 100 million sets of the game Monopoly have been sold since it was invented in 1935. Parker Brothers prints 18.5 *trillion* dollars in play money every year. That's more than all the real money printed by every country in the world!

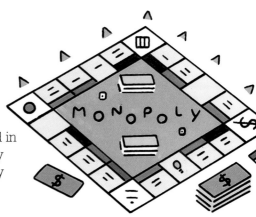

222

Hard on the hand!
In early games of baseball, nobody wore gloves. Being a catcher was especially hard. In fact, each team went through a few catchers during a game. Players started wearing gloves in 1875.

223

Slow pitch . . . In the first years of baseball, the pitcher wasn't allowed to throw the ball overhand. His only job was to give the batter an easy ball to hit.

What goes up . . .
Baseball's longest-lasting fly ball took years to hit the ground. Batted by Dave Kingman of the Oakland Athletics in 1984, the ball went so high that it lodged in the roof supports of the Minneapolis Metrodome. Years later, the ball was finally knocked down to the field, and was promptly sent to the Baseball Hall of Fame.

224

Keep your *eye* on the ball . . .
Joe Spring attempted a most difficult baseball catch in 1939. At the San Francisco World's Fair, he volunteered to catch a ball thrown from a blimp that was 800 feet straight up. Joe almost caught the ball, but it hit him in the face. He lost five teeth and was knocked out cold.

226

No elevators allowed . . .
One of the most bizarre races in the world takes place every year in New York City. It's a running race—right up the 1,550 steps of the Empire State Building! It's the hardest quarter-mile race on the planet!

225

Not so newfangled . . .
Early roller skates had five wheels in row—a lot like today's in-line skates.

227

THE WORLD

The Sky, the Stars, the Planets

228

Mercury

Rotate and revolve . . . A year is how long it takes a planet to go one full orbit around the Sun, and a day is how long it takes a planet to make one full turn on its own axis. One Mercury year is only 88 Earth days. And one Mercury day is almost as long— 59 Earth days!

229

Venus

Hey, I'm a planet! From Earth, Venus looks like a very bright star. The poisonous gases that surround Venus don't absorb much sunlight but bounce the light back into space. That's why the planet looks so bright.

230

Earth

Spaceship Earth . . . Right now, you are moving at 67,000 miles per hour. That's how fast the planet Earth travels around the Sun.

231

Mars

Real Martians? Mars is a cold, desert planet where wind and sandstorms sometimes cover the surface. Some scientists believe there may have been oceans and even life on Mars long, long ago.

232

Jupiter

Giant planet . . . Jupiter is so large that you could fit all of the other planets inside it and still have room for more. Jupiter has at least 16 moons orbiting it.

Shhhh!

233

News travels slowly . . . Using sensitive radio telescopes, scientists are hoping to pick up some evidence that there is other intelligent life in the universe. But they'd better be patient. Signals from the nearest star would take over four years to reach Earth, and signals from the other side of our own galaxy would need about 70,000 years.

234 Saturn

Saturn, here we come! In 1997, the unmanned spacecraft *Cassini* will leave Earth and journey 762 million miles to explore Saturn. It should take *Cassini* seven years to get there.

235

Ice rings . . . Saturn's famous rings are made up of trillions of chunks of ice— from tiny crystals to icebergs as big as houses.

236 UraNus

Long, long summer . . . How would you like your summer vacation to last for 42 years? That's how many Earth years one summer lasts on the planet Uranus.

Sky pizza . . . Io, one of Jupiter's moons, has more active volcanoes than any other known body in the solar system. All of those volcanoes have made Io's surface look like a pepperoni pizza!

237

239 PLUTO

The longest journey . . . Faraway Pluto is the only planet in our solar system that hasn't yet been visited by a space probe from Earth. Scientists have begun to plan ways to send a satellite out there to take a closer look. Telescopes have already revealed a moon they've named Charon, which is so large and so close to the planet that astronomers often call Pluto and Charon a double planet.

238 Neptune

Brrrrr . . . Icy Neptune is 2.7 billion miles from Earth. Neptune has at least eight moons. One of its moons, Triton, may be the chilliest spot in our solar system. The temperature can dip down to 391 degrees below zero.

BRRR R R !

240

Deep river . . . Even though the Nile River is longer than the Amazon River by 137 miles, the Amazon River holds three times as much water.

241

More than a blizzard . . .
Talk about a snow day! Six and a half feet of snow fell in one day in the Copper River Basin of Alaska in February 1963. Imagine the snowmen you could make after a snowstorm like that!

Lots of variety . . .
Some 1,500 different kinds of butterfly live in just one square mile of the Amazon rain forest. There are only 750 different kinds in all of the United States and Canada.

242

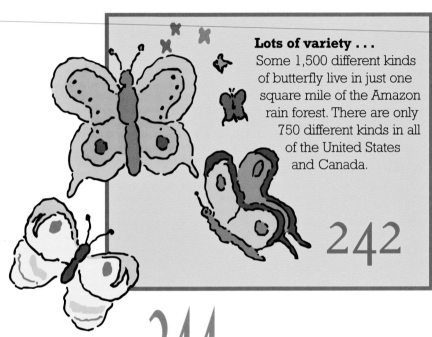

244

Too much trash . . .
An average American family throws away about one and a half tons of trash every year. Try to pick up a midsize car. Then you'll have a good idea how much trash that really is.

243

Breezy!!!
The windiest place on earth is Commonwealth Bay in Antarctica, where the wind can blow up to 200 miles per hour. Hold on to your hat . . .
and your car . . .
and your house . . .
and just about everything else!

246

Save a tree . . . About 220 million trees are cut down every year just to make the newspapers printed in the United States. Remember to recycle!

245

Garbage dump . . .
There is a mountain of garbage near New York City that is as tall as a 50-story building. It's called the Freshkills landfill on Staten Island, and over 15,000 tons of trash are dumped there every day.

247

Old stuff into new . . . Some winter jackets are made from recycled plastic soda bottles. Factories can turn old plastic into yarn that can be woven into clothes, carpets, and even sleeping bags.

248

Want some mustard with that?
A "garbologist" is a scientist who studies what we throw away and what happens to the things that end up in landfills. One garbologist found 10-year-old hot dogs buried deep in a landfill—and they had hardly decomposed!

YECCH!

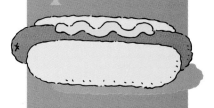

249

Stony bones . . .
The skeletons of billions of tiny sea animals called coral make up the Great Barrier Reef off the coast of Australia. Over 1,000 miles long, it's the largest coral reef in the world. That's a lot of little skeletons!

250

Oxygen factory . . .
The Amazon Basin in South America is the site of the biggest tropical rain forest on earth. It covers about a billion acres in Brazil, Peru, Venezuela, and Bolivia. This huge forest is thought of as "the lungs of the earth," because it produces much of the oxygen we breathe every day.

251

Life on the canopy . . .
Most of the animals in the rain forest live in the treetops. That's because most of the food is up there. The forest is so dense that the sunlight cannot get through to the floor of the forest. This dense covering of treetops is called the canopy.

252

Underwater mountain . . .

Mauna Kea in Hawaii is the tallest mountain on earth, but you can't tell by looking at it. Mauna Kea is more than six and a half miles tall, but only about two miles stick out above the ocean water. If you are measuring height starting at sea level, then Asia's Mount Everest is the tallest mountain.

253

Isle of sand . . .
The world's largest island completely covered with sand is Fraser Island, off the coast of Queensland, Australia. The island is one giant sand dune—more than 76 miles long!

254

Fungus humungous . . .
One of the largest living things on earth isn't an elephant, or even a whale. It's a fungus named *armilaria bulbosa*. It lives in a forest in Michigan and is more than 1,500 years old. It weighs as much as a giant blue whale and is as big as nine football fields.

255

Big brother sun . . .
Our Sun is so big that more than 1 million Earths could fit inside it. It looks small because it's more than 93 million miles away. The next closest star is 25 million miles away, so all the other stars look tiny!

256 **A one-continent world . . .**
If you had been alive 250 million years ago, you could have walked from your house to China without getting your feet wet. At that time, there was only one great landmass, which we refer to as Pangaea, or "all the earth."

Food Factory . . .
Since they can't move around, plants have to make their own food. They use a process called photosynthesis, in which they combine sunlight, water, and carbon dioxide to make sugar. Plants also make oxygen for us to breathe.

257

258

The hole truth . . .
For more than 24 years, scientists in Russia have been drilling a hole to learn more about the earth's structure. Today, the hole is more than seven miles deep . . . and they're still digging!

Mooning around Mars . . . Mars has two moons named Phobos and Diemas. These names mean "fear" and "terror." The moons of Mars aren't round like our moon. They look more like huge potatoes floating around the planet.

259

Even *grander* canyon . . .
The Grand Canyon is just a tiny hole in the ground compared with the Valles Mariners on Mars. This huge canyon is 2,500 miles long. That's almost long enough to stretch across the United States.

262

Lotsa lava! Mount Olympus, a volcano on Mars, is almost three times bigger than Mount Everest, our tallest mountain.

263

Ups and downs . . . When you are traveling aboard the space shuttle you get to see a sunrise every hour and a half.

264

Killer from space . . . Many scientists believe that dinosaurs were wiped out when a huge asteroid hit Earth. The dust from the explosion blotted out the sunlight. This killed the plant life, which left nothing for the dinosaurs to eat.

261

Weight problem . . . If you weighed 100 pounds on Earth, you would weigh almost three tons on the Sun.

265

Which end up? In space, you can sleep standing on your head. There is no feeling of up or down.

266

Heavy duty . . .
The Sun weighs two thousand trillion, trillion tons.
That's 2,000,000,000,000,000,000,000,000,000 tons!

267

When you wish upon a . . . meteor?
Shooting stars aren't stars at all. They are
meteorites falling to Earth.

268

**Light on
its feet . . .**
It takes sunlight
eight and one third minutes to
get to Earth. It is traveling at
the speed of light, of course—
or 186,000 miles per second.

269

Ulysses' travels . . .
Scientists are sending the space
probe *Ulysses* to visit the Sun.
Ulysses is the fastest–moving object
ever made by humans. It zips along
at seven miles a second— more
than 25 thousand miles per hour!
That's fast enough to travel from
New York City to San
Francisco in under seven
minutes.

270

No clippers . . .
Your fingernails
grow more slowly
in space.

271

The sky is falling . . .
One hundred tons of
meteorites fall to Earth
every day. Most fall in
the ocean. Some are as
small as a piece of dust.
You could be hit by one
and not even know it!

Smash!
The chances of an asteroid hitting our planet are slim. But scientists are exploring how they can protect Earth if they see one coming. One plan is to shoot bombs into space to blow the asteroid into tiny pieces before it crashes into us.

272

273 **Keen eyes . . .** Are your eyes good enough to see something 13 million trillion miles away? Astronomers say that on a very clear, moonless night, the Great Galaxy in Andromeda, called Messer 31, can be seen with the naked eye.

274

Flying snowball . . .
Imagine a snowball the size of a large city racing through space. That's what a comet is. When it flies by the Sun, the snowball melts a bit, and a trail of water and gas forms behind it, which can stretch for millions of miles.

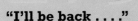

"I'll be back . . . ."
Halley's comet is the most famous comet in the sky. It just streaked by Earth in 1986. It will return in 76 years, in 2062.

277 **Bad omen?**
Long ago, people were afraid of comets and shooting stars. They thought they were unlucky or would bring bad news. In fact, the word *disaster* means "evil star."

276

No harm done . . . On May 19, 1910, the tail of Halley's comet brushed against Earth, but no damage was done. The tail was mostly gas and some icy dust.

278

Around she goes . . .
A year is the time it takes a planet to go all the way around the Sun. It is different for each planet. Of course, here on Earth, it takes about 365 days.

279

Making waves . . . Once, during ancient times, a landslide underneath the ocean made a wave that was 1,180 feet tall. That's almost as tall as the Empire State Building! The word used for a giant tidal wave is Japanese—*tsunami.*

280

Nosing out Neptune . . . For 20 of every 250 years, Pluto is closer to the Sun than Neptune. In fact, Pluto is closer right now— and will stay that way until 1999.

281

Whizzing water . . . A tidal wave can go 630 miles per hour. That's faster than a jet airplane!

282

Really deep . . . The deepest place on the earth is the Marianas Trench in the Pacific Ocean. It is 36,198 feet deep—that's more than six and a half miles straight down!

283

Continental drift . . .
The continents are all moving on the surface of the planet like huge rafts in the ocean. Every year, North America moves almost one inch.

284

Squashed circle . . .
The earth isn't completely round. It is flat at the North and South Poles.

FANCY PLANTS
& Fascinating Flowers

285
Super picker . . .
A man named George Adrian of Indianapolis, Indiana, once picked 366 bushels of apples in only eight hours. That's about 16,470 apples—or one apple every 1.7 seconds.

286
Mouths to feed . . .
In 1850, each farmer in the United States grew enough food to feed four people. Today, each farmer can grow enough to feed more than 80 people. That's because farming is now a very scientific business, with new machines, new ways of watering crops, and new disease-resistant crops. At this time only three of every 100 Americans are farmers.

287
Give me a ring . . .
Next time you see a tree stump or a freshly cut log, try counting its rings. Each year a tree is alive, it adds a new band of cells to the outer layer of its trunk. As the rings accumulate, the trunk gets wider.

288
Closing time . . .
Some plants, like crocuses and morning glories, close up their flowers in reaction to the cool night air. Once the sun comes back up and the temperature rises, the flowers quickly open up again.

289

Move over, Kermit!
Floating on a lily pad can be fun—as any frog can tell you. But South America's Victoria water lily has leaves so big and strong that small *children* can easily float on them!

290

Not just for kissing . . .
Mistletoe may look pretty hanging over a doorway during the holidays, but it can be a scary visitor for a tree. A mistletoe plant is a parasite—something that feeds on another living thing. It has been called the vampire plant because it sinks its sharp roots into the trunk and branches of a tree and steals its food.

291

Come on in! Can you imagine a tree so big that 20,000 people could stand in its shade at the same time? There is a banyan tree in India with the widest spread of any plant on earth. Four football fields could fit beneath its branches.

292

Not too thirsty. . .
Just as a camel stores water in its hump, a cactus stores water in its stem. The saguaro cactus of the American Southwest can store enough water to stay alive for three years without rain.

293

Puff balls . . . Which clocks don't tell time? Dandelion clocks. That's what we call the fluffy white balls on a dandelion gone to seed. When the wind —or you—blows on them, the seeds look like tiny parachutes being carried away on the breeze. When they land, the wind and rain help them work their way into the soil, and in just a few weeks, there are more dandelion plants.

294

The better to see you with?
Potatoes have eyes, but not for seeing. Potato "eyes," those little white dimples that grow if you leave them around for a while, sprout buds that can be planted to grow new potatoes.

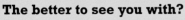

Fancy Plants & Fascinating Flowers

295

Wildlife weather report . . .

A rhododendron can tell you the temperature outside. During warm weather, its broad leaves open flat and stick nearly straight out from their branches. As it gets colder, the leaves begin to droop and curl. At 20 degrees Fahrenheit, the leaves are tightly curled and hang almost straight down.

296

GENERAL SHERMAN

Biggest ever . . .

Giant sequoia trees are the largest green plants and the heaviest living things that the earth has ever known. The biggest one of them all is named the General Sherman tree. Scientists think that General Sherman is about 3,500 years old, and they estimate that it weighs more than 6,000 tons.

297

Broccoli bouquet . . .

Did you know that some of the vegetables we eat—like cauliflower, broccoli, and artichokes—are really flowers? You can prove it. If you put broccoli stalks in a glass of water and wait a few days, the buds will open into pretty yellow flowers!

298

Spreading palms . . .

African raffia palms have the largest leaves in the world. One of these feather–shaped leaves can be more than 65 feet long. The leaves are made of tough, durable fibers, and Africans often use raffia to weave mats and other useful things.

Watch out for falling fruit!

The largest fruit of all grows on the jackfruit tree in Asia. One jackfruit can weigh 65 pounds. How much do *you* weigh?

299

300

Seed-spitter . . .

The squirting cucumber plant doesn't wait for birds or insects to help spread its seeds. Like a blown-up balloon, the plant builds up gas and pressure inside its flowers. When the seeds are ready, the flowers burst and the seeds spray out—landing as far as 40 feet away!

301

Lighting up the night . . .

The Japanese fungus *Mycaena lux-coeli* glows so brightly that it can be seen from 50 feet away in the dark.

302

Which mushroom is which?

Some mushrooms are good food, and some are poisonous and deadly. Ancient Romans depended on specially trained mushroom pickers to know the difference.

303

Corn energy . . .

Ethanol is a kind of alcohol made from corn. When it's mixed with gasoline, it makes a fuel called gasohol. Cars and trucks that burn gasohol instead of plain gasoline make less pollution.

304

Beautiful but deadly . . .

Some plants are best left alone. Eating the leaves of a deadly nightshade can kill a person. The plant is also called belladonna, which is Italian for "beautiful woman."

305

Don't touch!

Poison ivy makes us itch because of a chemical in its leaves and stems called urushiol. The amount of urushiol that would fit on the head of a pin is enough to make 500 people itchy.

Where do the foods we eat come from?

How is your favorite breakfast cereal made?

307

Fields of Wheaties . . .
Cereals are grain crops, and the name comes from the Greek goddess Ceres, protector of the harvest. Corn is made into cornflakes, wheat into wheat flakes or shredded wheat, rice into rice puffs, and oats into oatmeal or oat crisps.

306

Sweet stuff . . .
Most of the sugar in or on your cereal comes from the sugarcane plant, a member of the grass family. A sugarcane plant can grow to be 20 feet tall! We also get some of our sugar from the sugar beet, a juicy root that grows under ground.

308 A bark with a spicy bite . . .
The cinnamon sticks you use to spice up your hot cider are curled pieces of bark from the trunk of the cinnamon tree.

Jellytree?
Jelly, jams, marmalades, and preserves are made from fruits like grapes, oranges, and apples–and they all come from plants.

309

WHAT'S IN A PEANUT BUTTER-AND-JELLY SANDWICH?

310

I'm not nuts! A peanut isn't really a nut. It's a seed like a pea or a bean. But it looks like a nut, and it and tastes like a nut, so there's no sense trying to change its name now! Peanut butter, made from ground–up peanuts, was first made and sold in St. Louis in 1890 by a doctor. He advertised that peanuts were "very nutritious." They are— in moderation.

311

Plants at the movies . . .
Chocolate and popcorn come from plants. Seeds from the fruit of the cacao tree are used to make hot cocoa, chocolate milk, and all kinds of chocolate candies. Coffee is made from ground-up beans—the fruit of the coffee plant.

312

Pow!
Popcorn pops for the same reason a balloon explodes when you blow it up too much. There's a tiny bit of water inside each popcorn kernel. When the kernel gets hot, the water turns to steam and expands inside the shell. When the kernel can't stand any more pressure, it **pops** open.

313

It's corn-tained in everything!
A modern American supermarket sells about 1,300 different foods that contain some kind of corn as an ingredient. Cornstarch, for example, is used in pancake syrup, ice cream, and canned soup. Isn't that corny!

314

Underground treat . . .
Ever wonder why root beer is called *root* beer? Simple: That special flavor comes from the *root* of the sassafras tree.

315

Food for thought . . .
Hot dogs, hamburgers, ice cream, and the cheese on cheeseburgers don't come from plants . . . but they do come from animals that *eat* plants. All of these foods come from cows that eat grass, hay, and grain.

Can you think of a food that doesn't start with plants?

316

Looks like magic . . . Some mushrooms grow in circles on the ground because of the way they spread their tiny seeds, called spores. People sometimes call these circles "fairy rings," because they look like an enchanted place where fairies might dance.

A fungus is among us . . . It's not green. It doesn't have any leaves. It doesn't send down any roots. But it does grow in the ground, especially after a rain, and it definitely *is* a plant. Give up? It's the mushroom.

317

Come to dinner . . . The Venus flytrap has a pair of spiny leaves that are wide open . . . most of the time. When a fly or a spider is attracted to the sweet nectar between the leaves—*zap!* They snap shut and trap the insect. Then strong fluids in the plant dissolve the dinner guest, turning it into food. The Venus flytrap is found only in the swamps of North and South Carolina.

318

319

Fit for a king . . . The powerful Aztec king Montezuma was perhaps the first chocoholic. His people in ancient Mexico discovered how to make delicious foods from cacao seeds, and he loved to sip rich chocolate drinks from his fancy golden goblets.

321

Or maybe you'd like a drink? The pitcher plant looks friendly to insects, mice, and even frogs. It looks like a tall, thin glass of water. The trick is that once critters climb inside, they can't climb out. Like the flytrap, pitcher plants are carnivorous, which means they eat meat.

320

Watch out! A sundew plant has leaves covered with sticky hairs that smell good to passing insects. When an insect lands, it gets stuck. The hairs quickly fold over the trapped insect and the plant "eats" it.

322 Hey . . . Hay!

When grass is covered with deep winter snows, farm animals can't get to their dinner! They can't wait until spring to eat, so every fall, farmers cut down tall grasses and let them dry in the sun. The dried grass is stored in big blocks called bales. This "hay" makes good eating for cows, horses, sheep, and goats all winter long.

323

Pretty on purpose . . .
It's not an accident that flowers and fruit blossoms are beautiful and smell good. Those bright colors and pleasant scents attract insects, birds, and other animals. When these visitors move from blossom to blossom, they spread the pollen around. This helps produce fruit and more seeds, so new plants can grow.

324

Sour flower . . .
Smelling the flowers isn't always pleasant. More than 90 percent of all flowers have either a nasty odor or no smell at all.

325

Long-livers . . .
There are bristlecone pine trees in California that have been growing slowly and steadily for over 4,600 years. That makes them some of the oldest living things on the earth.

THINGS THAT GO

...on the ground

326

Roll it! A very, very long time ago, there were no wheels of any sort. Nothing rolled. Need to move that log? Drag it. Need to get that pig to market? Make it walk, or carry it. No bicycles, no cars, no trucks, no skateboards, no wagons. The best guess is that the first wheels were made from round slices of tree trunks about 5,000 years ago.

327

Wheel trouble . . . The idea of the wheel probably developed in a lot of different places. But it only caught on in places where animals like horses or oxen were available to do the pulling. If a man had to pull a heavy cart himself, the wheel might not seem like such a great idea.

328

Heavy burden . . . Today, in places where there are no roads—like sandy deserts or high in the mountains—people still use animals such as donkeys, camels, and llamas to carry heavy loads.

Go cart . . . The first high-speed vehicle was the chariot. A chariot had two wheels with spokes, and it was pulled by one or two horses. The driver rode standing up. From about 1,500 B.C. on, whenever ancient kings went to war they might have had as many as 30,000 chariots charging at one another on a battlefield.

330

329

Tough biking . . . The first bicycle was just two straight-ahead wheels with a seat between them. There was no way to steer the front wheel and no pedals to make the back wheel turn. You just sat on the seat and pushed on the ground with your feet to make it go. And the brakes? Same deal! Use your feet!

331

Don't run over that fish!
Who would be silly enough to ride a tricycle underwater? A team of 32 divers, that's who. They pedaled a tricycle almost 177 miles underwater. It took them three days, three hours, and 20 minutes. And why did they do it? Probably so books like this would tell about it.

Tough going . . .
The Iditerod International Dog Sled Race in Alaska is one of the most difficult races in the world. A driver and a pack of dogs travel 1,137 miles through bone-chilling cold and blinding blizzards.

332

333

Carriage craze . . .
Until 1900, almost everyone rode on horses or in horse-drawn carriages. Did you know that the word *car* is short for *carriage*?

334

Does it come with a ladder?
In 1870, an English inventor made a bicycle with a large front wheel and a small back wheel. It was nick-named the pennyfarthing, after the smallest and largest copper coins used in England at that time.

CARS/TRUCKS

Prairie schooners . . .
The American pioneers took huge flatbed wagons and turned them into traveling houses called covered wagons, by stretching heavy canvas over a framework of bent wooden poles. A white-canvased wagon rolling across the prairie reminded someone of a sailing ship rolling over the waves, so "prairie schooner" became the nickname for a covered wagon.

335

336

Slower than a horse . . .
The first car to run on gasoline was built in Germany in 1885. It was called a Benz, and it looked like a giant tricycle. Top speed? Just 12 miles per hour!

337

How engines run . . . Today, horse-drawn carriages have been replaced by vehicles powered by internal combustion engines. In a car engine, a mixture of fuel and air is burned. As the mixture gets hotter it explodes and pushes on the pistons, which turn the crankshaft. This makes the car's wheels go around.

339

Long warm-up . . .
The Stanley Steamer was a car powered by a steam engine—just like old-fashioned trains. It could go 30 miles an hour, but it took half an hour for the car to build up enough steam to start moving.

338

Eight-legged bus . . .
The first city to have buses was Paris, France. In those days, buses were pulled by horses and carried only seven people—eight, if you count the driver!

340

Fire fighters . . . There are different kinds of fire engines designed to do different jobs during a fire. The hook-and-ladder truck carries the long ladder that can rescue people or lift a water cannon up as high as 100 feet. The pumper truck can push 1,500 gallons of water per minute through the long, cloth-covered hoses.

Dump it! Trucks with big, open-topped boxes on the back were invented to carry loads of stuff like rocks, dirt, sand, and firewood. These trucks had to be unloaded with shovels or by hand. Then someone had the bright idea that the box could be built so that the whole thing would tip up and drop the load in one big pile. And that was how the dump truck was invented.

341

34²

Tractor travel . . .
A group of young farmers from Great Britain traveled 14,500 miles by tractor. They left England on October 18, 1990, and arrived in Zimbabwe, Africa on March 4, 1991.

343

Hold on to your hat!
A jet-powered car called the Thrust 2 holds the record for the fastest mile traveled on land. It went nearly 633.5 miles per hour over Nevada's Black Rock Desert in 1983. To slow down after its run, the driver released parachutes from the back end.

344

Mansion on wheels . . . The largest camper in the world is five stories tall and weighs 240,000 pounds! It has eight bedrooms, eight bathrooms, and a garage with space for four cars. It was built for a very, very rich Arab sheik.

UNDERGROUND

345

Big city, big subway . . . A subway is a train that travels underground. New York City has the biggest subway system in the world. It has 469 stations and almost 232 miles of track. Up to 5 million people ride it every day.

TRAINS

346

Hooves of steel . . . The steam locomotive was called the "iron horse." Can you guess why? Hint: It was made of iron, and it raced across the prairies like a horse.

347

Flying trains . . . An electric train in France called the *train à grande vitesse* (train at a high speed) can go as fast as 186 miles per hour. An even faster passenger train built by the Japanese is the "bullet train" which travels at 219 miles per hour!

348

And even faster ones! Ever notice how magnets can be turned to push away from each other? That's the idea behind a new trackless train in Japan. It's called the Maglev train, which is short for "magnetic levitation." The whole train floats on a magnetic "cushion," a powerful, invisible magnetic field. Because the train doesn't touch anything there's no friction, and that makes great speed possible. Test runs have hit speeds near 250 mph!

349

It's a train! No, it's a tractor! Early tractors, like the Case Steamer, looked like train engines puffing across the fields. They had giant iron wheels and tall smokestacks. Today, farmers drive gasoline-or diesel-powered tractors.

...In the Air

BALLOONS

Full of hot air . . . What makes a balloon go up? Gas or heat. Some balloons lift off because they are filled with a gas that weighs less than the air outside the balloon. This makes them rise through the air like a bubble through water. Hot-air balloons get their lift because hot air weighs less than cooler air. When a special burner heats the air inside the balloon, it rises because the air outside the balloon is cooler.

350

351

Farmyard fliers . . . The first flying machine was created in 1872 by two brothers from France named Joseph and Jacques Mongolfier. It was a large bag, 35 feet around. The brothers burned straw under the bag, and the hot air made it rise a mile in the air. The first passengers were a duck, a sheep, a rooster, and finally a person, Pilatre de Rozier, on October 15, 1783.

352 **Down we go . . .**
There are two ways to bring a hot-air balloon down. To come down quickly, hot air can be released from the top of the balloon. To go down more slowly, the pilot just stops using the burner. The air cools gradually and the balloon floats back to earth.

353 **Floating across the sea . . .**
In 1978, three American men became the first people ever to cross the Atlantic Ocean in a balloon. The *Double Eagle II* was filled with helium gas, and it took six days to travel from Maine in the United States to a little town just outside Paris, France.

AIRSHIPS

ZEPPELINS/BLIMPS

354

Slow ride . . . Riding in a blimp is very different from riding in an airplane. Blimps fly closer to the ground and move a lot more slowly. The average speed of a blimp is 28 to 40 miles per hour—slower than a car on the highway.

355

The last zeppelin . . .
The largest and most famous zeppelin was the German-built one called the *Hindenberg*. It could carry 70 passengers in luxury and cross the Atlantic Ocean in two days. Unfortunately, the *Hindenberg* used hydrogen gas, which catches fire easily. In 1937, the *Hindenberg* caught fire, exploded, and crashed to the ground in Lakehurst, New Jersey.

356

Power balloon . . .
Balloons go where the wind pushes them, but motorized airships, or dirigibles, can fly any direction the pilot chooses. The two kinds of dirigibles are blimps and zeppelins. Blimps, like the ones that hover above football stadiums, are like giant, hollow balloons blown up with helium gas. Zeppelins are much larger than blimps and have a stiff frame or skeleton that holds the gas bag in place. Zeppelins are not made anymore.

357

Fuel saver . . . A blimp can fly for nearly a week on the same amount of fuel that a jet plane uses just to taxi down the runway and take off. That's because the helium in the blimp takes care of keeping it in the air, and all the engine has to do is push it forward.

358

Seemed like a good idea at the time . . .
The tower at the top of New York's Empire State Building was built as a place for airships to land and tie up. The building was completed in 1931, and during the next six years, there were so many airship disasters that the landing tower has never been used.

PARACHUTES

Soft landing . . .
The idea for a parachute probably came from an experience with an umbrella on a windy day. Invented in France in the late 1700s, parachutes got their first real test in 1783, when Louis-Sébastien Lenormand dove off a high tower and landed safely on the ground. The first parachutes were made from canvas. Next came silk, a much lighter cloth. Today's parachutes are made from nylon, a tough, light, man-made fabric.

359

Gimme a brake! NASA's space shuttle, some super fast jets, and even some race cars release parachutes to slow down after they've landed. Without these drag chutes, the brakes would be ruined very quickly.

360

361

Gliding on air . . . Gliders are planes with no engines. They have narrow bodies, long, thin wings, and are made of light materials so they can glide and rise up on thermals–hot-air currents rising from land that has been heated by the sun. Eagles, hawks, and giant condors can do this, staying aloft for hours without ever flapping their wings.

AIRPLANES

362 **History at Kitty Hawk . . .**
The first airplane flight was made on December 17, 1903. Orville and Wilbur Wright had been working on their motor-powered plane for years. Orville became the first person in the world to successfully fly a heavier-than-air vehicle. The flight lasted less than 12 seconds, and the plane flew only about 120 feet from takeoff to landing.

363

A real lift . . . What makes an airplane fly? Something called lift: air pushing up on the bottom of a plane's wings. The wings on an airplane are shaped so that when the plane moves forward through the air, this lift starts pushing up on both wings. As long as the plane moves forward fast enough, there will be enough lifting force under the wings to keep the plane up.

364

From pull to push . . . The first planes had propellers like the blades of an electric fan. They spun around and pulled the plane through the air. Today, most planes have jet engines. Jet engines have a big opening in the front and a small opening in the back. Air gets pulled in the front by a powerful fan called a turbine, and then gets pushed out the back. Because the hole in back is smaller than the hole in front, the air goes faster out the back. This creates something called thrust, which pushes the jet plane along.

365 **Whirly bird . . .**
The helicopter has a long history. Leonardo da Vinci discovered the idea and sketched it before the year 1500. In 1907, a French inventor named Paul Cornu was able to lift himself off the ground for a few seconds in a machine with rotating wings. But the first real helicopters did not appear until 1938 in Germany, and in Russia in 1940.

366

Up and away . . .
What takes off like a helicopter and flies like an airplane? A new kind of aircraft called the X-wing. It uses rotors to rise like a helicopter, but once it's up and flying forward, the rotor stops and acts like regular airplane wings.

367 **Faster than sound . . .** SST stands for supersonic transport, airplane travel that is faster than the speed of sound—which means flying faster than 670 miles per hour. Supersonic planes have long, needle-like noses and wings that sweep backward. This design helps the plane slice through the sound barrier.

...On the Water

368

Crunching along . . .
Icebreakers have extra-strong hulls that can't be broken or pierced by ice. They also have extra-powerful engines. Some seaports would have to stop all shipping during the winter if icebreakers did not keep a lane open for regular ships to use.

369

Sea, see?
Ancient Romans painted eyes on the fronts of their boats to make sure the boats could "see" where they were going.

370

From float to boat . . .
Wood floats. Early humans found they could move on the water by sitting on logs. The first boats were hollowed-out logs called dugouts.

371

Water wings . . .
Hydrofoils are special underwater fins shaped like airplane wings, down along the sides of a boat. When the ship moves forward at a certain speed, the hydrofoils lift the boat up so that only the hydrofoils are still in the water. The rest of the boat is above the waves, gliding along, using less energy and having a smoother ride.

372

Smooth sailing . . . Why would anyone want to put a wing on a ship? To save fuel. Wing sails work like airplane wings. They create a flow of air that helps push the ship forward. Ships with wing sails use one-third less fuel than ships without them.

374

Very cutting . . .
If you've ever tried running through the water, you know that it pushes against your legs and slows you down. Boats have the same problem. To help with this, ships have pointed bows that help them cut through the waves more easily.

373

A sub called *Alvin* . . .
The floor of the ocean is one of the last unexplored places on earth. Today, scientists can get to the bottom and study in a special kind of submarine called *Alvin*. Alvin has robotic arms that can collect sand and rocks and other things from the bottom of the world.

...Underwater

Things That Go Into Space

Want to fly to the moon?

A new kind of rocket called the Delta Clipper could take you there someday. Today's rockets gradually get rid of their empty fuel tanks and engines, called stages, so they can go fast enough to fly into orbit. But rockets like the Delta Clipper and the NASP will stay in one piece and be reusable. Some scientists think ordinary people may be able to fly in them by the year 2005.

376

Tails of the space program . . .

Did you know that America's first astronauts were monkeys? Their names were Able and Miss Baker. The two monkey-nauts blasted off in 1959, and they proved that living creatures could survive space travel.

377

Reusable rockets . . . NASA's space shuttle was the world's first reusable spacecraft. Can you name the five space shuttles? *Answer: Columbia, Challenger, Discovery, Atlantis, and Endeavor.*

378

Ticket into orbit?

NASA is planning a national aerospace plane, the NASP. It will take off and land like a plane, but it will fly up through the atmosphere into a low Earth-orbit, like the space shuttle's. The NASP will be able to carry lots of passengers, and fly between New York and Tokyo in just two hours.

379 **Around the world 16 times a day . . .** By the year 2000, the space station Freedom should be ready for astronauts to move in to. Their new home will circle the Earth every 90 minutes, in an orbit that is 250 miles from the planet.

380 **Sock catcher . . .** When you opened a drawer to look for socks, you wouldn't expect them to float up into the air. But if you lived on the space station, they would. That's why drawers on Freedom will be topped with nets that hold things in place.

381

Some assembly required . . .
Space station Freedom is designed to be assembled in pieces. The space shuttle will make many flights to carry all the pieces to the giant station.

382

Turned around . . .
If you live in a space station where there is no gravity, no weight, you don't automatically know which surface of a room is the floor and which is the ceiling. So inside space station Freedom, floors will be painted one color and ceilings another.

383

Taxi! Once Freedom is completed, the space shuttle can ferry astronauts and supplies back and forth from Earth to the station— the most expensive taxi service ever!

384

Emergency exit . . . Ships have lifeboats. What about space stations? Docked alongside space station Freedom will be an ACRV—that's short for Assured Crew Return Vehicle. If it's ever necessary to get astronauts back to Earth in a hurry, the ACRV will be ready go.

REMARKABLE PEOPLE

and Crazy Characters

385 Dino–might . . .

According to *Forbes* magazine, Barney the Dinosaur was one of the richest entertainers of 1994. The purple creature made $84 million. No other dinosaurs made the list.

386 Short but soaring . . .

You don't have to be Michael Jordan to slam dunk a basketball. Little guys can dunk it too. Spud Webb, an NBA player who stands only five feet seven inches, can leap high enough to dunk the ball into the 10–foot rim.

387 Living dolls . . .

Barbie and Ken are real people. In fact, they are brother and sister. The owners of Mattel toys used their daughter Barbie's name for the popular doll. And when she needed some company, they picked their son Ken's name for her boyfriend doll.

388 Dear Mr. President . . .

Abraham Lincoln didn't grow his famous beard until after he was elected president. A young girl wrote him a letter and told him that if he grew a beard, his long face wouldn't look so sad. He took her advice—and the rest is history.

389 Shoe biz . . .

You could say that Imelda Marcos, the wife of the former president of the Philippines, likes shoes . . . a lot. Her huge collection included 1,000 pairs of black high-heeled shoes —all exactly the same.

390

Long faces . . . The tallest presidents of all are Washington, Jefferson, Lincoln, and Teddy Roosevelt. Their heads alone are over 60 feet tall . . . on Mount Rushmore.

392

Lucky Lindy . . . Charles A. Lindbergh flew the first solo airplane flight across the Atlantic Ocean in May 1927. He flew 3,610 miles from New York to Paris, in 33 hours, 29 and a half minutes.

391

Worldwide well-wishers . . . The most crowded wedding ever had more than 701 million guests. When Prince Charles and Lady Diana of Great Britain got married in 1981, 2,700 people came to the church, 1 million lined the streets outside, and 700 million watched on television.

393

Boy king . . . In 1331 B.C., a nine-year-old boy named Tutankhamen became the pharaoh, or king, of Egypt. King Tut died nine years after he took the throne. His treasure-filled tomb was discovered 3000 years later, in 1922.

394 **Scads of siblings . . .**
Imagine having 68 brothers and sisters! That's how big the family of Fydor Vassilet of Russia was. His wife gave birth to 69 children, the most ever. This included 16 sets of twins, seven sets of triplets, and four sets of quadruplets!

396 **Private paradise . . .**
Michael Jackson has his own amusement park and zoo. There he can ride his own Ferris wheel, carousel, or bumper cars. Or he can visit his animal friends at the zoo, including zebras, ostriches, llamas, giraffes, and even zonkeys, a combination of zebras and donkeys!

395 **Left out?** Left-handed people can have a hard time with things such as scissors. In some parts of the world, it is even against the law to eat with your left hand! Only one out of every 10 people is a lefty, but there have been lots of famous lefties, including Alexander the Great, Michelangelo, Leonardo da Vinci, Babe Ruth and Judy Garland.

Remarkable People

THERE'S NO PLACE LIKE HOME

397 **Prez on wheels . . .** Theodore Roosevelt was the first U.S. president to ride in a car. In 1902, he took a spin in a purple-lined Columbia Electric Victoria.

398 **One big lady . . .** Stretching eight feet, her index finger would tower over the tallest basketball players. Her big toe is as big as a small car. From toe to torch, the Statue of Liberty stands 152 feet tall and weighs 450,000 pounds.

399 **Shoe-seum . . .** Dorothy Gale's ruby slippers from *The Wizard of Oz*—the ones Judy Garland wore in the movie— can be seen any day at the Smithsonian Institution in Washington, D.C.

400 **Dot's a fact . . .** Louis Braille went blind after an accident in 1816. He later developed a special alphabet, made up of raised dots, to help blind people read and write easily. This alphabet is called Braille and is used now by millions of blind people around the world.

401 **Handled with care . . .** Jimmy Carter is the first U.S. president to have been born in a hospital.

402 **Moving pictures . . .** Bill Gates is one of the richest people in the world. He made his money creating computer programs. Gates lives in a fantastic house built into a hill outside Seattle, Washington. The paintings throughout his house may look real, but they are actually computer images. Gates can change any of the paintings in an instant.

403 **The hole story . . .** Doughnuts have holes in them because a boy in Maine didn't like soggy doughnuts. Fifteen-year-old Hanson Crockett Gregory noticed that though the outside of his doughnut was cooked and brown, the middle was always soggy and raw. In 1847, he poked a hole in a doughnut with a fork, which helped cook the entire doughnut.

405

Getting credit . . .
The *Pietà* in St. Peter's Cathedral in Rome is the only statue that Michelangelo ever signed. One day, he overheard someone say that another artist had created it. That night, he sneaked into the church and signed his name.

404

Fabulous feats . . . Blondin was one of the greatest daredevils that ever lived. He was a tightrope walker who walked across Niagara Falls on a wire. The first trip took him 22 minutes. Over the years, he repeated the feat and added something more difficult each time. At different times, he crossed carrying a man on his back, walking on stilts, and with his feet in a sack.

Nellie's travels . . . In 1889, a lot of people were talking about the book *Around the World in 80 Days*. The idea of traveling around the globe in such a short time was a wild one. Nellie Bly, a gutsy reporter, would do anything for a story. She sailed on boats, jumped trains, rode camels and elephants, and finally traveled around the world in just 72 days, 6 hours, and 10 minutes. Today, a plane can fly around the world in a matter of hours.

407

406

Quiet concert . . .
John Cage was a composer who dared to experiment. One of his most famous pieces is called 4'33". A performer would sit at the piano and not play a note for four minutes and 33 seconds. The audience was encouraged to listen to the silence and hear the music in the sounds around them.

Goose music . . . We're not sure who the real Mother Goose was. Some people believe that she was Elizabeth Foster, who married a man named Isaac Goose in 1693. She lived in Boston and often sang songs to her grandchildren. Her son-in-law published these songs in a book called *Songs for the Nursery: Mother Goose Melodies.*

408

Remarkable People

Love, Beatrix . . .
Beatrix Potter wrote *The Tale of Peter Rabbit* in a letter to the son of a friend. It was later published as a book.

410

409

To tell the tooth . . .
The *Good Ship Lollipop* couldn't set sail without Shirley Temple's two front teeth. In the 1930s, the eight year-old was such a big star that she wore tiny false teeth in movies until her new ones grew in.

Tell me a story . . .
Five-year-old Christopher Robin Milne heard the adventures of Winnie-the-Pooh, Piglet, and their friends every night when he went to bed. His father, A. A. Milne, created the Pooh stories based on his son's stuffed bear and other toys.

411

HUNNY

Cosmic accident . . .
In the past 500 years, only 12 people that we know of have been hit by meteorites. Mary Ann Hodges of Alabama is the only American to have been hit by one. She was sitting on her couch when a meteorite the size of a baseball crashed through her roof and hit her in the leg, causing only a bruise.

412

413

Famous cub . . .
The original Smokey the Bear was rescued from a fire in New Mexico in 1950. Forest rangers found him clinging to a charred tree, and named him Smokey. He lived at the National Zoo in Washington, D.C., wore a forest ranger cap, and became the mascot for forest fire prevention.

414

415

Hoppy ever after . . .
A Frenchman named Charles Perrault doomed Cinderella to wear glass slippers. The story of Cinderella is hundreds of years old. In the original story, her slippers are made of fur. The old French words for "fur" and "glass" sound the same. When Perrault wrote the story down in 1697, he used the wrong word, and Cinderella has been squeezing into glass slippers ever since.

Tiny Tom . . . Tom Thumb was the world's most famous midget. He stopped growing when he was only six months old. When he was a teenager, he stood only 25 inches tall and weighed 15 pounds.

416

Tissues anyone? Donna Griffiths of Great Britain sniffled her way to the world's longest sneezing spell. She sneezed for 978 days—that's more than two-and-a-half years! She sneezed over one million times in the first year!

417

Born to box . . . In 1943, one-and-a-half-year-old Muhammad Ali accidentally knocked out one of his mother's teeth with a left jab. Twenty years later, he won the world heavyweight boxing championship.

418

Young Genius . . . Wolfgang Amadeus Mozart wrote his first piano concerto in 1761, at the age of five.

420

Passion for paint . . . Henri Matisse was one of the greatest artists ever. He loved to paint so much that when he was older and couldn't get out of bed, he painted on the ceiling with paintbrushes on the ends of long poles!

421

Spaced out . . . The first woman in space was a Russian named Valentina Tereshkova. She blasted off on June 16, 1963. The next morning, there was no word from Valentina. Everyone was worried that something had happened to her. An hour later, she finally came on the radio. She had just overslept!

419

Young aviator . . . An 11-year-old girl from Pennsylvania named Victoria Van Meter made history in 1993 when she became the youngest female to fly across the United States. It took her four days to fly from Maine to California in a small plane called a Cessna 172.

422

Ride, Sally, Ride . . . Sally Ride was the first American woman in space. She took a six-day trip aboard the space shuttle *Challenger* in June 1983. Many woman have since done the same.

Inventors

423 Yum!

Ruth Wakefield accidentally invented the most popular cookie in America: the chocolate chip cookie. Ruth worked at the Toll House Inn in Massachusetts. She was baking chocolate cookies one day but ran out of baker's chocolate. She decided to break up pieces of chocolate and add them, thinking they would melt and mix into the cookies. They didn't, and the Toll House, or chocolate-chip cookie, was born.

424

Favorite treat . . . One out of every two cookies made in America is a chocolate-chip cookie.

425

Sticky stuff . . . A walk through a patch of burrs inspired George de Mestral of Switzerland to invent Velcro. He was picking burrs off his sweater and decided to take a closer look. He put one under the microscope and saw tiny hooks. He created Velcro in the same way, with lots of tiny hooks on one strip and small loops on the other.

426

Springy thingy . . .
Richard James of Philadelphia accidentally invented the Slinky™ in 1945, when he knocked a coil of wire off a shelf. He was stunned when he saw the spring "walk" down from the shelf to a book to the floor. His wife came up with the name "Slinky."

427

Easy to eat . . . The sandwich got its name from the earl of Sandwich, who didn't want to stop playing cards to eat. He told his servants to stick meat inside two slices of bread so that he could keep a hand free to play cards.

428

Waffly good . . . Charles Menches was selling ice cream at the 1904 St. Louis World's Fair. One hot day, he ran out of dishes. A man selling waffles at the next booth gave him an idea. He rolled the waffle into a cone and scooped the ice cream inside. The first ice-cream cone was called a World's Fair Cornucopia.

429

Possibili-tea . . . According to Chinese legend, tea was discovered by the emperor Shen Nung in 2737 B.C. He was boiling water outside when a few leaves from a nearby tree blew into the pot. When he started to remove the leaves, he smelled a wonderful aroma coming from the water, and changed his mind.

430 Satisfied customer. . .

Potato chips were invented to satisfy a fussy eater who thought his french fries were too thick. George Crum was a chef in Saratoga Springs, New York, in 1853. When someone complained that his fries were too thick, Crum shaved the potatoes so thin that you couldn't even pick them up with a fork. Everyone loved them, and today the potato chip is one of our favorite snacks.

431

Hello, hi-fi . . . Thomas Edison invented the record player in 1877. He recorded the poem "Mary Had a Little Lamb."

Remarkable People

432 Trickster . . .

According to legend, Leonardo da Vinci's teacher was once painting a woman's portrait outside. The teacher needed to go somewhere and told Leonardo to keep leaves from blowing onto the canvas. While he was gone, da Vinci painted a leaf on the woman's nose. When the teacher returned he saw the leaf and scolded his student. But when he went to remove the leaf, he saw it was a painting. He knew then that Leonardo would be a great painter.

434 Marble master . . .

Michelangelo said that when he worked on a sculpture, he wasn't carving a figure out of the marble. Instead, he was setting free something that was trapped inside the stone.

435 Big Cheese . . .

William Howard Taft was the largest president. He weighed over 300 pounds and had to have a special bathtub installed in the White House. After he served as president, Taft became a judge on the U.S. Supreme Court.

433 Graffiti guy . . .

One of the most famous modern artists started out painting graffiti. Keith Haring painted colorful pictures on the walls in New York City subway stations. His paintings now hang in museums around the world.

436 Forever joined . . .

Chang and Eng, the world's most famous Siamese twins, were born in Siam (now Thailand) in 1811. We call twins who are connected "Siamese twins" in honor of them. Chang and Eng toured in the circus and then moved to North Carolina to be farmers. They spent three days a week at each twin's farm. The twins married two sisters and had 22 children. They died in 1874, within two hours of each other.

437 Mini-Madison . . .

James Madison was the smallest president. He stood only five feet, four inches tall, and weighed less than 100 pounds.

438

Wire-walker . . . Phillipe Petit wanted to go from the top of one of the World Trade Center towers to the other. Most people would ride the elevator down to the ground floor, walk over, and ride up again. Phillipe had a better idea: He strung a wire between the two and walked across.

439

Lots of dots . . .

A painter named Georges Seurat used lots and lots of dots to create some of the most beautiful paintings ever. Painting with dots is called *pointillism*.

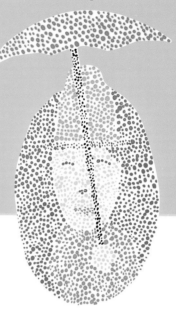

440

One-horse town . . . Alexander the Great was a famous military leader. He rode a wild horse named Bucephalus, who never let anyone but Alexander ride him. When the horse died, Alexander built a city in his honor. The city of Bucephalus still exists in India.

441

Big talk . . . Paul Bunyan, the legendary lumberjack, was larger than life. According to "tall tales" he stood taller than the trees, and his footprints filled with water and created the 10,000 lakes in Minnesota!

442

He wants *you* . . . The real Uncle Sam was a merchant from Troy, New York, named Samuel Wilson. When Wilson was shipping food to the U.S. army during the War of 1812, he wrote the initials "U.S." on each package. His friends spread the word that the "U.S." stood for Uncle Sam. Now Uncle Sam represents the government of the United States.

443

Historic day . . . John Adams and Thomas Jefferson both died on July 4, 1826, the 50th anniversary of the Declaration of Independence. Adams's last words? "Thomas Jefferson still survives."

WEIRDER THAN WEIRD

444

Zebra prints . . .
A zebra's stripes are as unique as your fingerprints. No two zebras have the same pattern of stripes.

445

Talented tongue . . . When a snake sticks its tongue out, it isn't being rude. It is just smelling the air. A snake uses its tongue for smelling, touching, *and* tasting.

446

Man-size birds . . . Prehistoric penguins were six feet tall. Today, they are only about half that size.

448

Bubble power . . .
An armadillo swallows air so that it can float on the water.

447

Mooo . . . By the way, all cows are girls.

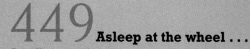

449 **Asleep at the wheel . . .**
An albatross is a huge seabird that can sleep while it is flying through the air at 25 miles per hour.

450

A number of its own . . .
Each of the twin towers of New York City's World Trade Center has its own zip code!

451

Jumpy!
A penguin can jump six feet out of the water onto an iceberg.

452

Long trail . . .
If you put all of your blood vessels end to end, they would stretch over 60,000 miles—that's almost two and a half times around the earth!

453

Info superhighway . . .
Messages from your brain travel at speeds of up to 240 miles per hour on high-speed nerve networks inside your body.

Pygg tale . . .
The first piggy banks were not in the shapes of pigs. The name comes from a material called pygg, which is a lot like clay. In the Middle Ages, people often saved money in jars made of pygg. In the 1800s, someone made the first pygg jar in the shape of a pig.

454

Weirder Than Weird

455 Bridge in the desert . . . These days, to cross the original was crumbling, and about to fall down, so someone bought it,

Pedal pushers . . . Merry-go-rounds were once powered by bicycle pedals on the horses. The faster everyone pedaled, the faster the carousel went.

456

457
Frogfall . . . It never actually rains cats and dogs, but it can rain frogs. A whirlwind or waterspout can pick up water from a riverbed that contains frogs' eggs. As the water is blown through the sky, the eggs hatch, and the next rainfall includes tiny frog tadpoles along with the raindrops!

Sleepyheads . . .
If you want to buy a present for koala bear, get it a pillow. Koala bears sleep as much as 18 hours a day.

458

460

459

The Whitish House?
The president's house, the White House in Washington, D.C., was always called the White House, but it wasn't always so white. It was built from grayish white limestone, and compared with the red brick buildings all around it, it was the "white" house. During the British invasion of 1814, the house was burned. It was then painted a bright white to hide the burn marks.

It's not sweet and it's not a bread . . .
If you ever see the word *sweetbreads* on a menu, you should know what you're ordering. Sweetbreads are chunky bits of meat from inside a cow's throat.

London Bridge you need to took it apart, and rebuilt it go to Arizona. The bridge in sunny Arizona.

461

Something up their sleeves . . .
During the Middle Ages, people didn't have pockets to hold their belongings. They would store things in their sleeves or down their shirts. Sleeves became so large and puffy that a person could have put a whole bag of groceries inside one.

462

Skeleton skaters . . .
There are Scandinavian stories about skating that go back before the year 200. The blades on the earliest ice skates were made from the bones of small animals. In fact, the English word *skate* comes from the German word for leg bone—*schake*.

That's 48 kneecaps!
Each one of the eight legs of a daddy longlegs spider has 6 joints!

463

464

Canine islands . . .
The Canary Islands aren't named for a bird, but for a dog. When Romans arrived there, they noticed how many dogs were on the island, and called it *canaria insula*, "the island of dogs." Only later did the little yellow bird found there become known as a canary.

465

Com-moon-ication problem . . .
Sound is carried in waves through the air. Since there is no air on the moon, two people standing on its surface just a foot apart would have to use radios to talk to each other.

466

Wait until I write it out . . .
Maybe we should have parades and fireworks on August 2. The Declaration of Independence was voted on and adopted on July 4, 1776, but it wasn't signed until August 2, almost a month later. It had to be rewritten on parchment before it could be formally signed.

467

1, 2, 3 . . . If you counted out loud from one to one billion, you would end up in a rocking chair. It would take you 95 years!

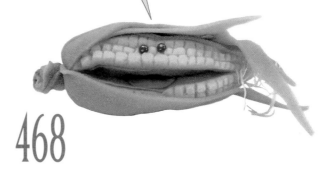

Corny! More than half of the corn in the world is grown in the United States.

468

470

What did you say?
Papua, New Guinea, is an island nation about the size of Texas. The 4 million people who live there speak more than 700 different languages and dialects.

469

Now, where was I? If you visit the Greek island of Mykonos, you'll probably get lost. To confuse pirates, the town of Mykonos was designed as a confusing maze and all of the buildings were painted white.

471

Goof-a-roo . . . When Captain Thomas Cook first landed in Australia, he saw an odd-looking animal. It stood as tall as a human, jumped on powerful legs, and carried its young in a tummy pouch. When Cook asked a native what the animal was called, the man said, "Kan-ga-roo," which in his language meant, "I don't understand you."

472

What would happen if they could vote? Kangaroos outnumber people in Australia 10 to 1.

473

Pressure suit . . .
Without a space suit on, an astronaut's body would explode in outer space. Our bodies are built to be contained by air pressure, which is created by the weight of the atmosphere that surrounds Earth. The space suit has its own pressure, a portable atmosphere for human beings.

474

Ms. Vampire . . .
Only a female mosquito bites. If she doesn't get some extra iron from a drink of blood, she can't lay her eggs.

475

Snipping surgeons . . .
In the old days, barbers cut hair *and* did medical operations. In fact, the red-and-white-striped barber pole represents a bandage wrapped around a person after an operation.

476

Very jumpy . . .
Every year, thousands of frogs from all over the world are flown to Calaveras County, California, for the world frog–jumping championships. No toads allowed.

That's Italian . . .
Even though blue jeans are as American as apple pie, the word *jeans* comes from Italy. The kind of weave used for the cloth to make jeans originated in Genoa, Italy.

477

The beat goes on . . .
Can you think of anything that you will do almost 3 billion times in your life? That's about how many times your heart will beat. It beats about 72 times every minute.

479

478

Still some air in there . . . Your lungs are never completely empty, even when you think you have blown out all the air.

481

Airborne messages . . . Kites were invented in China more than 3,000 years ago. Legend has it that some of the first kites were used by armies to send messages and signals over hills and across huge battlefields.

482

Horse pooped . . . Polo is a tiring game, especially if you're the horse. Polo ponies get so tired that a player may ride as many as 12 different horses during one game!

480

Fantastic flier . . . Most birds use their wings to flap and glide through the air, but the hummingbird flies more like a helicopter. Hummingbirds can fly up, down, forward, backward, hang in midair, and even fly upside down! This is because their tiny wings can beat up to 70 times per second.

484

My how you've grown! Giant Squids never stop growing. They can grow to 50 feet long.

485

Someone spit in my soup! One soup in Asia is bird's nest soup. It's made by boiling the nest of an Asian swift. The yummiest part of the nest is considered to be the saliva that the bird uses to hold the whole thing together!

483

Paw preference . . . Just like people, dogs and cats favor a right or left front paw. Like us, dogs tend to be right-pawed. Cats, on the other paw, tend to be lefties.

487

Bony babies . . . Babies have 300 bones and adults have only 206! As people grow larger, some of their smaller bones fuse together to form larger and stronger ones.

486

Outnumbered . . . For every person living on earth, there are 200 million insects!

489

Swim like a fish . . . Our fastest swimmer can just barely beat a goldfish. The fastest we can swim is five miles an hour. A goldfish can swim four miles an hour.

490

Just relax . . . Quicksand doesn't drag you down. In fact, it is easier to float on quicksand than on water. What drags you under is your struggle to get out. If you just relax and lean back, as you would do in a swimming pool, you will float to dry land.

488

Waves instead of potholes . . . In Venice, Italy, the main streets never need repaving. That's because they are made of water—and called canals. The city consists of 120 islands in the Lagoon of Venice. To get around, people use motorboats or beautiful, hand-rowed taxi boats called gondolas.

Weirder Than Weird

492
Tight fit . . .
Some 150 years ago, kids didn't have to worry about putting their shoes on the right feet. Before the 1860s, both shoes were the same!

491
Clunky but dry . . .
Dutch people wear wooden shoes because a lot of their land is wet or underwater. Wooden shoes are better than leather ones if you have to walk on soggy ground a lot.

493
Hide your eyes . . .
In 1430, judges in China started wearing dark glasses to hide their eyes, so no one could see what they might be thinking during a trial. The modern habit of wearing sunglasses outdoors started in this century, when airplane pilots found the need to wear special glasses to block out glare.

494
Glug, glug . . . You will drink 16,000 gallons of water in your lifetime.

495
Spinner . . .
The name spider comes from the old English word *spinnan* which means "to spin."

496

"We work here . . ."

In parts of Greenland, the only dogs allowed are sled dogs.

Gobblers . . .

Each Thanksgiving Day, Americans eat 50 million turkeys.

497

499

Submerged snooze . . .

Seals can sleep underwater and come up for air without even waking up!

498

Chirp means chill . . .

A cricket's song slows down as the weather gets cooler. You can guess the temperature in Fahrenheit if you count the number of chirps in one minute and divide that number by 40.

How about a hug?

Not all starfish have five arms. The basket starfish can have as many as 50 arms. A starfish can even grow a new arm if it loses one.

501

Humble beginnings . . .

In 1955 Jim Henson made the first Kermit (who was not yet a frog) from an old coat that belonged to his mother. He added two halves of a Ping Pong ball for eyes, and the soon to be world famous muppet character was born. Here, a modern Kermit (left) sits next to the original Kermit (right).